GO TO THE DESERT

DESERT

Healing from Alcohol:

A Spiritual Perspective

Casey Crespo

Book Coach: Dinah Laprairie

Editor: Annette Quinn

Cover design by Casey Crespo

ISBN: 9798286026319

Printed in the United States of America

First Edition

Website: www.caseycrespo.com

Email: clcrespo27@gmail.com

Contents

Although this book explores these ideas through the lens of alcohol, I believe the same insights and tools can be useful for addressing any other coping mechanisms that no longer serve you.

<u>Why Are We Here?</u>

I thought I would be a party girl forever. I spent 20 years drinking like it was a full-time job, and have seen all the drama, debauchery, and fuckery that comes along with it. It kept me on autopilot, like a robot, just going through the motions of a life I was barely participating in. Alcohol was my all-purpose tool— my escape hatch, my emotional duct tape, my way of avoiding all the parts of my life I didn't want to face.

The decision to stop drinking alcohol is a fucking brave one. It takes guts to question your relationship with alcohol, and the fact that you're here means you're already stronger than you think. This is the book I wish I had while going through it. It's a reminder that **_YOU ARE NOT ALONE_**— and what's waiting for you on the other side isn't just about drinking less or quitting— it's about finding freedom, clarity, creativity, and a kind of joy you may have forgotten even existed.

This book is for those who feel like outcasts in both the sober world and the spiritual world.

If you've ever sworn off alcohol for a couple of weeks— maybe even made it through a dry month— only to find yourself circling back to the same old patterns, then this book is for you. You tell yourself it's not *that* bad. You're still showing up. Still functioning. Still holding it all together. From the outside, no one would suspect a thing. But inside? You know. You *feel* it. A quiet voice in you says, *If I could just get this out of my life, my whole world would expand.* Maybe you've already stopped drinking, but you're still searching for the better life sobriety promised— and wondering where the hell it's hiding. Maybe you've looked into AA like I did, and it felt too heavy or serious, too extreme, or didn't resonate. You're not at rock bottom, but you are stuck. You know there's more for you. You can sense the power just beyond the fog. This book is your bridge to it.

If you're feeling dull and lifeless, my goal is to guide you toward inspiration and curiosity, helping you live in alignment with your full vitality. If you're feeling trapped in a drinking cycle (or any other coping mechanism) you can't seem to break out of, may this book help you illuminate how to escape so that you may feel the freedom you desire. If you feel disconnected from your true self or don't even *know* what you need to move forward, I can encourage you to take baby steps until you are confident in making bigger changes, navigable with the tools suggested in this book. If you're feeling scared or awkward about not having alcohol as a crutch, I am here to empower you to be comfortable enough in your skin to let your authenticity shine. If you feel like strict quitting programs are too rigid or intense for you, this book guides you to your own inner compass while encouraging self-compassion and self-love. If you're afraid of what's hiding underneath the mask of alcohol, I'm here to offer encouragement to hug your shadows to release them. If you have a spiritual curiosity but may not know how to connect, this book will help you develop your own tools for a deeper connection.

You don't need another set of rules. You don't need to be shamed or told what's wrong with you. You need a safe space to be seen. This book is your invitation to examine your relationship to alcohol without judgment. Everything I share comes from lived experience, not perfection— just truth, compassion, and the deep knowing of what it's like to be right where you are. I'm here to be a mirror, not a guru.

This book was written over a year and a half, right in the thick of the biggest upheaval of my life. I stopped drinking after a major breakup. I left New York. I walked away from my job without a backup plan. Every page is a breadcrumb from that messy middle— where I wasn't sure who I was without alcohol, without the city, without the old routine and my coping mechanism of choice. You're not reading some polished before-and-after story. You're walking through the fire with me. This is what it looked like to strip everything down and start to build a life I didn't want to escape from.

This isn't just about quitting alcohol— it's about dragging your autonomy, vitality, and true self out of the corner where they've been gathering dust. You're choosing to swim against a whole ocean of societal bullshit and *think for yourself*— for your mental, physical, and emotional survival. And let's be clear: that's no small thing. It's badass. You're choosing to stop hiding from yourself, even when it would be easier to stay numb. No one quits drinking and stays the same person, just minus the cocktails. It doesn't work like that. You're going to change — *you're supposed to.* And while the process can feel awkward, messy, and uncomfortable as hell, the ripple effect in your life is real, undeniable, and better than you can imagine right now.

When I stopped drinking, I was forced to ask myself, "What do I truly need to be happy?" Booze gave me cheap, fast highs that kept me in a state of numb complacency, blocking me from considering long-term goals and dreams that would set me up to live a life I wouldn't need alcohol to enjoy. This transition can feel incredibly overwhelming, but you don't have to have it all figured out to take the next logical baby step. In the *Support Tools* section of this book, you will find suggestions on navigating your new life— the exact things that helped me when I was right where you are. Nudges in the right direction. Guidance to listen to yourself. Clues to discovering your true nature and purpose.

I'm not here to list all the scary statistics about alcohol; if you're here, then you already know. I'm not here to tell you what to do or how to live your life or even suggest that it's a magic formula for you. Instead, together, we will transmute so-called "negativity" into raw power, using it as fuel for growth, self-discovery, and healing. This is about stepping into our highest potential, free from the haze of alcohol, and embodying the clarity, confidence, and resilience that have always been within us. We are taking our power back, rewriting our stories, and alchemizing our lives into something extraordinary.

If you are trying to cut back on alcohol, for most, it's not as simple as not picking up a drink. You must become comfortable enough in your skin to not have the desire to reach for a drink anymore. Can't imagine that yet? That's ok, it will come. I am here to encourage you to examine WHY you want that drink in the first place. And most of the time, that deep introspection is not fucking pretty. We can keep putting it off, but we can't hide from ourselves forever. Eventually, we realize that we have no choice but to be authentic. And by being authentic, we take our power back from alcohol. It is a bold move, so congratulations on being here.

Suppose you take the time to honestly examine your connection to alcohol through the lens presented here, dive deep into the reflection work, and explore the research. In that case, I have no doubt that you will unlock a newfound sense of freedom, lightness, and curiosity about your world. An alcohol-free life isn't about restriction— it's about expansion.

Spirituality, and a greater connection to Source, Universe, God (or whatever you call it), cannot be separated from this healing process. If you know me personally, you may not be aware that I am a spiritual person, but I am deeply drawn to various spiritual concepts as a source of guidance through life, and this book reflects that. The spiritual growth I have experienced through healing from alcohol overindulgence has been undeniable. Spirituality and deep healing are an intensely personal journey, and let me tell you— it's not all unicorns and rainbows. This isn't some fluffy "love and light" book. I'm here to keep it real: if you want true transformation, you must be willing to walk through the darkness first. It's impossible to experience the highs without equal and opposite lows. That's the nature of duality and part of the ascension process. Think about all the lows you've experienced with alcohol, and know that it is possible to experience the opposite joy regularly instead.

You may already have an internal guidance system that works for you. Spirituality is a vast smorgasbord of intriguing choices; some are classic and time-tested, others bold and relatively new. Whatever your personal needs or interests, use your inner knowing to take what resonates and leave what doesn't. It's up to us to determine the tools that resonate with us the most, based on the support we need at any given time.

The key here is that we accept the full spectrum of the journey without labeling dark times as "negative." You can *always* spin a "negative" experience into something positive— lessons learned, where you ended up, or who you met. If I hadn't basically marinated myself in booze for 20 years, gotten a master's degree in self-destruction with a minor in questionable life choices, I wouldn't have written this book, and I wouldn't have the privilege of helping *you* right now! Nothing is wasted. Even your biggest fuckups can be fuel for something beautiful. It's about perspective.

I prefer to call myself *mostly sober*. I do not identify as an alcoholic or an addict, nor do I consider myself entirely sober. These labels feel too rigid, final, and limiting. I believe labels can limit our ability to fully embrace our power. Labeling ourselves as an alcoholic or addict often carries negative and even punitive connotations, implying that we've made a "mistake" somewhere along the way or, worse yet, that we're somehow defective or doomed to failure, or because "I'm a THIS: (insert label here)." Consider for a moment: if you identify as an alcoholic or addict, could it, by definition, *reinforce* a negative self-image, keeping you tied to your past and potentially making it harder to move forward? It might also suggest that even something as relatively benign as drinking kombucha with a tiny percentage of alcohol could lead to a slippery slope of returning to harmful and excessive behaviors, like throwing all good intentions out the window and heading straight to the liquor store. This way of thinking can be dangerous because it implies that if you are labeled as an alcoholic, then actions like these are to be *expected*. Could holding such an expectation serve as an *excuse* to get drunk or relapse?

I'd rather free myself from the label and any built-in expectations that come with all labels. Don't try to put me in a box. My experiences, along with the lessons I've learned, have shaped me into who I am today. That said, if the label feels empowering to you, then by all means, use it. This is your journey, and you get to build your toolkit with the things that work for you.

Any ascesis (the practice of self-discipline or self-denial, undertaken for growth in some way) helps to have a clear goal of why you are doing it. Personally, my most motivating factor was my brain health. My memory was terrible, and I could feel my brain turning into a sad, gray mush. I was truly curious what I was capable of without alcohol as an influence. And here I am writing a book. But even if you don't have a goal in mind, the benefits of not drinking will still be undeniable, and you will make room in your life for all sorts of positivity to enter. The removal of the energy given to alcohol (before, during, and after drinking) clears the path for gifts from the universe, just waiting to reach you. Aren't you curious what they are?

I'm not a therapist or a doctor— I'm just someone who's been through it. Nothing in this book is meant to replace professional help. What I *am* here to offer is a real, honest approach to the *harm reduction* of alcohol, with plenty of room for self-love and self-acceptance. If alcohol has taken up too much space in your life, I want to show you how to take some of that space back— bit by bit— using practical tools, mindset shifts, and raw, unfiltered stories. We'll walk through a series of *Craving Scenarios*— those familiar moments and situations where the urge to drink hits hard— and break them down to get to the real need underneath. Because here's what I've learned on the other side: when you face the true need behind the craving with truth and compassion, the pull to drink loses its power. You don't have to white-knuckle your way through healing. You just have to get honest.

~ ~ ~

I'm not going to sit here and pretend that I've got it all figured out— because I don't. But what I can say with certainty is that

I'm closer to where I want to be now, without alcohol, than I ever was with it. After two decades of consistent drinking, it's been incredibly difficult to untangle all the ways alcohol has been woven into nearly every aspect of my life. The journey has been complex and challenging, but it's also shown me that there's so much more available on the other side. It's a slow unraveling of old patterns, relationships, and mindsets. And as I continue to grow, I've realized that there's nothing wrong with not having all the answers. It's about trusting the process and allowing myself to evolve at my own pace.

I won't sugarcoat it— it's incredibly tough, boring, and lonely at first, especially during those first three months. But trust me when I say it does get better, and it gets easier. Alcohol had been tied to nearly every aspect of my life, whether I was actively drinking or dealing with the aftermath. You can't rip it out and expect life to snap into a Zen montage immediately. Your body and mind are catching up to the rest and recovery it didn't get while under the influence of alcohol. I encourage you to take the time to do your research on how long it takes for your body and mind to heal from regular alcohol use. The healing process— along with getting to know a whole new "you" takes time, it's some of the most worthwhile time you'll ever spend.

Feelings of impatience and frustration of not feeling better instantly can feel like hopelessness, and maybe you think, "what's the point?" and suddenly your willpower feels paper-thin. Some may choose to call it a "relapse," but I'd rather think of it as just a messy experiment— a lesson that shows me where I'm still growing. Every stumble has pulled me closer to who I really am.

Don't feel like you must read this book cover to cover. If a chapter title piques your interest, feel free to go there— like a choose-your-own-adventure book. This is a relatable reference guide, a tool to support your decision to step away from alcohol, wherever you are on your journey. Take what helps and leave the rest. You are the only one who knows what's best for you. You always have your own inner wisdom (or guidance from your higher self) available to you. It's always there, just waiting for you to tap into it. Only you can decide what's best for you.

Be patient and loving with your body and mind, giving them the time and space they need to heal. It has been abused by poison and needs time to realign and balance. You're now facing the trauma that alcohol once helped you numb, and you can no longer hide from yourself. This journey forces you to be completely authentic, unapologetically human. You're learning to give yourself permission to truly feel your feelings and work through them— no more distractions. Remember, breakdowns often lead to breakthroughs. You are capable. You're much stronger than you think.

The more we learn to trust our own inner guidance, the more we can relax into the truth of who we are. When we embrace our true selves, without judgment or the need to fit into someone else's expectations, the need for alcohol as a coping mechanism begins to fade. Authenticity dissolves resistance, freeing us from the constant battle to numb or escape from reality. It invites us into a state of flow and ease, where we can navigate life with greater clarity and self-acceptance. The deeper we connect with our authentic selves, the less we feel the urge to hide behind anything that dulls our light.

"It has been said that the hardest and easiest thing in the world is simply be yourself."

-Richard Rudd, The Gene Keys

Part 1: The Story Behind This

Getting "Mostly Sober"

You always hear the same tired getting sober story— the total rock bottom, life in shambles, then boom: full sobriety, perfect life, cue the happy ending. But that's not how it goes for most of us. It sure as hell wasn't my path. The truth is, there's a whole messy, confusing, in-between space when you're trying to drink less, figure shit out, and not fall apart. That gray area is real, and not enough people talk about it.

There was always a nagging voice in the back of my mind that would tell me to drink less. I used to brush it off, drown it out, pretend it wasn't there. But deep down, I knew— it was my gut, my inner truth, trying to get my attention. I flat-out ignored that little voice for about 20 years, until it became strong enough and loud enough to take action. I could spend the rest of my life wondering what I could have achieved professionally if alcohol hadn't been involved, or what kind of relationships I could have built if they hadn't revolved around drinking. But we must offer ourselves grace and acceptance for the paths our lives have taken. There are no mistakes. We haven't done anything wrong. We learn, we grow, and we are here now.

I can't say I ever hit a "rock bottom" changing point. I never got a DUI, blew out any relationships, ruined any jobs, ended up in the hospital, or anything like that. However, I was prone to accidentally hurting myself while drunk.

My closest "rock bottom" incident was at a basement club in Atlanta called The Music Room, which happened within the same month as dealing with a stalker, and a crazy exposure to carbon monoxide at work. It felt like Atlanta was trying to kill me. Anyway, I went upstairs to say goodbye to a friend. It was raining outside, and the entryway was wet. Upon returning downstairs to join the party, my foot slipped on the top stair, and I tumbled, *hard,* down the entire flight of very unforgiving wooden stairs. I hardly felt it because I was fuckin wasted. It happened in slow motion, and I had no choice but to surrender to the unstoppable momentum— like I was caught in a washing machine with hard as fuck edges. At the bottom, despite lots of attention to my well-being from several *very* concerned people, I insisted I was fine to keep dancing.

Someone who saw it came over to tell the person I was with that I probably needed to go to the hospital or at least go home. After a few minutes of assessing my body and feeling a large bump forming on my head, I decided to leave. My bottom two teeth were chipped, I had a puncture wound from God knows what in my knee that has caused some weird numbness to this day, I had a bump the size of a golf ball on my forehead, and that blood settled in my eye causing a black eye, and various other bruises.

I bought purple eyeshadow to match my other eye to the black eye that developed a few days later, because I had to go to work and didn't want to explain my embarrassing story. I could hardly believe I didn't have any broken bones or, worse, wasn't dead from this accident. I was so incredibly lucky. Of course, I didn't want to admit how drunk I was to take responsibility for this accident. I made up other reasons it happened, like my shoes had no tread, it was raining and slippery, it could have happened to anyone, etc.

I kept drinking steadily for another five years. It's wild how many red flags we're willing to ignore— like the universe is straight-up screaming, "HELLLOOOO, THIS IS NOT OKAY," and we stuff our ears and keep doing the same old shit.

What warning signs have you been pretending not to see?

~ ~ ~

I don't identify with being "sober," it sounds so final and harsh. By this point, you may not be surprised to learn that I don't like rules very much. I don't like structure or routine. I think it kills magic in life. I relate to the element of water very much (as half of my astrological chart is water signs), going with the flow of things and deciding with my emotions and intuition what to do in the moment. If someone offers me a Sauvignon Blanc from Marlborough or a beautiful floral gin, I might decide to have a sip or glass, and I won't beat myself up about it. For me, it was important to break the *habitual unconscious act* of seeking out and buying alcohol. If I choose to have an alcoholic drink now, I recognize and respect the power of the poison. But the more time that goes by without it, the less I even want it.

Alcohol is a highly addictive substance, and when I learned from a scientific perspective podcast that my brain is just doing its job when it responds as such, it changed my perspective from "I have an addictive personality," to "I am just responding to an addictive substance that I am consciously consuming." Most of my experience with attempting to regulate how much I'll drink in a night does not work for me. If I say, "I'll just have two," then by two drinks in, my inhibitions and self-control are significantly lowered, making the willpower to keep the promise to myself much more difficult. It takes up much less headspace if I decide before going to an event that I will remain alcohol-free for the night. Most of the time, that approach is much more freeing than dealing with the internal dialogue between the "alcohol demon" and myself. I think it's amazing that some people can moderate and stop at one or two— more power to them.

Just as the word "sober" can mean many different things to many people, so can the word "moderation." The inherent nature of moderating an addictive substance is an uphill battle for me, and choosing to be *mostly* abstinent from alcohol has given me the best success. In addition, the more time that passes from my heavy drinking days, the easier it is to moderate.

Is it easy for you to moderate? Has your capacity for moderation changed over time?

~~~

With sobriety, there's often so much emphasis on how long exactly, down to the day, that you've been sober. While that works for many people, personally, I don't like rules. We are going for *harm reduction* here, not complete and rigid adherence to total sobriety. We are humans, not robots with on/off switches.

I think of it this way: When I was a heavy drinker, I drank almost every day. But in my first year of being mostly sober, that relationship with alcohol was essentially flipped. When I was drinking, I was probably alcohol-free for no more than 3 weeks a year, which means I drank 94% of the time. In my first year mostly sober, I was alcohol-free for 94% of those days. And where I come from, 94% is an A! That's a pretty fucking epic accomplishment for me. I refuse to start over with a "day one" if I have a glass of wine. I'd rather focus on the big picture, my overall goals, and celebrate the positive changes and how proud I am of shifting my lifestyle.

I've always thrived on the fringes of society and have had a slightly rebellious nature, and I think that's one of the traits that led me to stick with a mostly sober lifestyle, as counterintuitive as that may seem. Maintaining a fully functioning brain is one of the most rebellious things you can do. It enables you to question and critique everything— what you were taught, whether it still serves you, and if societal norms are truly beneficial to you or just conformity for someone else's benefit. Are you merely following the herd or contributing to your community in a meaningful way, in alignment with your values? Being fully conscious means you cannot operate on autopilot in a job or relationship that isn't fulfilling because you're keenly aware and in touch with your emotions. Are we truly living if we don't scrutinize every aspect of our lives, including what we consume?

The herd mentality is real, and it's one of the biggest things that keeps people stuck. It's that pull to go along with what everyone else is doing, even if deep down, you know it's not working for you. Most people don't stop to question the rules they're living by— they follow the crowd because it feels safer, easier, or more comfortable than standing out. Alcohol is reflected in the exact same way. But let's be honest: comfort doesn't equal growth.

When you're constantly looking around to see what everyone else is doing, you lose touch with your own truth. You silence your gut. You play small. And yeah, it might keep things feeling familiar, but it also keeps you trapped. Real change? That happens when you start thinking for yourself— when you stop asking for permission and start choosing what works for *you*. That's when shit starts to shift.

When you're the only one not drinking in a room full of people who are, it can stir up all kinds of weird energy. People might get awkward, defensive, or even a little too curious, like your choice not to drink is somehow a mirror they didn't ask for. It's wild to watch. You start to see just how deep the grip of social norms and peer pressure really goes. Even when people *know* alcohol can mess with their bodies, minds, and lives, they still reach for it. That tension between knowing better and doing it anyway? That's where the truth lives.

When I got mostly sober, it was an accident. I had been "sober curious" for a while in 2022. I could feel my brain turning to sad gray mush, my memory was getting bad, I was not as sharp, my energy was low, and I was, in general, not a very happy person unless I was drinking. After 20 years of drinking multiple beverages nearly every day, I was finally warming up to the idea of not drinking so much. There was a significant barrier, though.

The relationship I was in at the time was an extremely alcohol-enabling one. We both fuckin loved it, and we had a "great time" together. Until it wasn't fun anymore. He had to be responsible at a young age, so he didn't get the typical party time that most people in their 20s get, and he was making up for it in his late 30s. And I understood that and respected that this was his path. For me, on the other hand, party culture was starting to get old and tired to me, as I had been doing it since I was 15.

That mismatch turned into fights and this weird power dynamic, like one of us was on some high horse while the other was still in the thick of it. It got toxic fast. Screaming at each other over the dumbest shit, arguments going nowhere because we were too drunk to communicate what was even wrong. I remember that towards the end, we got into a huge, stupid fight over our opinions about those dried seaweed snacks. I was so upset I stayed with a friend that night, and she reflected at me, "sounds like it's not about the fuckin seaweed snacks." And she was right. In reality, the root of our problems was our unhealed trauma, soaked in booze, and therefore amplified and distorted.

The more "sober curious" I got, the more I could see what alcohol was doing to my partner, and the more apparent the negative influence it was having on my personal choices. Alcohol was keeping him trapped in a place in life he was unable to climb out of. It kept him complacent, in an endless loop of hopelessness stacked on top of dead ends and brick walls. It was the same fucking traumatic stories over and over again, and it was excruciating to watch him relive over and over.

I'm a highly spiritual person, so naturally, I gave him spiritual suggestions because that's been my solution while navigating tough times. All of it would be quickly shot down and ridiculed. After delicately walking on eggshells for years around the topic, I finally had a chance to sit down with him and put on a guided meditation, and I was *so excited that* I may have finally been breaking through. Not five seconds into the meditation, he freaked out and told me to turn it off. To this day, I still don't understand why. The way he reacted, you would think I was trying to do an exorcism on the devil. That spiritual part of me got swept to the side and covered up with alcohol the entire relationship, and has taken some time to feel comfortable with again. After realizing I couldn't help someone who wasn't ready to help themselves, I decided I couldn't watch the self-sabotage and suffering anymore, and I removed myself from the situation. I wanted to be healthy with him, but I couldn't force it, and I had to take care of myself first. I now know I need my relationships to positively influence me, because my willpower isn't strong

24

enough to watch my partner drink every day while trying to stay sober.

That breakup was a major driving force behind my change, and afterwards, without the alcohol-enabling feedback loop, it was so much easier for me to cut back tremendously. I hadn't fully committed to quitting drinking yet, but I was taking more extended breaks. The cycles during that time seemed to be 2-3 weeks of *no* drinking, then 1-2 weeks of drinking. Finally, I was *sober* more days than days I would drink each month. This switch was HUGE for me. I was already *mostly* sober! I was consciously changing my relationship with alcohol, warming up to the idea of cutting out even more. This part of the journey— the messy, in-between, not-quite-sober-but-trying phase— doesn't get talked about enough. If your story isn't the classic cold-turkey, all-or-nothing version, then yeah, there's gonna be a blurry, uncomfortable transition. Be kind to yourself. Be patient. You're unlearning years of patterns, and that shit takes time. Remember to look at your *overall* progress and not get too caught up in the parts that may feel like a step back.

I took a spur-of-the-moment solo trip to Hawaii's Big Island to spend Christmas and New Year's. I had just finished working as Head Tailor on a movie called "Imaginary Friends" and was newly single, so I was embracing that new independent feeling again. Except it was different this time— instead of being a newly single party girl, I was newly single and taking my power back from alcohol and a narcissist ex. I had plenty of family I could have been with, but I've never been a fan of forced holiday traditions, so I decided to adventure on my own. Besides, this was going to be my first Christmas ever where I was planning not to drink, whereas years prior it was an excuse to start at 10 am, thank you, baby Jesus. It felt right to me to disrupt the pattern without being tempted by the same situations, traditions, and people. I'm sure you can relate.

I booked a sacred plant ceremony with a Shaman on the Big Island of Hawaii for New Year's Eve. I had heard great things about ayahuasca supporting healing journeys, so I was initially searching for that. During my research, I came across a Shaman who created a psychoactive plant brew using native Hawaiian plants. This brew is similar to ayahuasca, but less intense, lasting shorter, and, to my understanding, has a softer, more loving vibe than ayahuasca. I was going through some significant life changes, so intentionally participating in a spiritual ceremony on the biggest party night of the year seemed like a great way to shake things up and start my year fresh. I had *no* idea what a huge influence that experience would eventually have on me.

The instructions leading up to the ceremony included cleansing your body by avoiding alcohol for two weeks and eating clean food. The recommended alcohol-free period was two weeks, but the directions strictly said, "absolutely no drinking 2 days before the ceremony." I was on vacation, so naturally, I was drinking. I managed to stop on Christmas Day, which was one week before the ceremony. Even though this was already a big step for me, I still felt ashamed that I couldn't make it for the full two weeks as the instructions suggested.

The plant medicine was beautiful and carried a warm, loving energy that felt like the universe and I were exchanging a warm hug. It felt a lot like a low dose of ecstasy, and the *wanting to get fucked-up* part of my brain wanted more. Glad the shaman was there controlling the dosage, or I probably would have drunk the whole pitcher and barfed my brains out. I only barfed once! During my journey, I doodled mandalas, and I wrote three beautiful messages from the plant teachers that I refer to often:

1.   "I forgive myself. You have done nothing wrong, ever."

We CANNOT beat ourselves up for doing something we think is "wrong." It is only wrong if you label it as such. Let your past actions serve as a guide for your future actions. There is always a positive side to even the most negative things. Flip the narrative. Focus on the positive.

2.   "Nothing real can be threatened!"

If you live in your truth, the universe will always take care of you. Authenticity is so important.

3.   "Fuck structure."

Routine and rules are a slow death. Live your life the way you want without any outside influence. Go with the flow of life; be water.

After the ceremony, I decided to continue my alcohol-free journey indefinitely. I knew deep down I probably had a problem I didn't want to admit to fully. It was time for a break to show my body the respect it deserves.

Over a year later, the Shaman from the plant ceremony visited me in a dream and told me very clearly and authoritatively to **"Go to the Desert."** One of the ways I interpreted this advice was to continue to stay dry from alcohol since my commitment to being mostly alcohol-free began at the time of his ceremony. There was so much more built from this vivid, profound, yet short dream, and I can't wait to tell you more in the last chapter.

~~~

I've never been big on rules, so I didn't draw a hard line in the sand with drinking. No strict "I'm never drinking again" declarations. Still, I've stayed mostly sober for about two years now. Yeah, there've been a few times I've had a drink— or a few— and every single time has taught me something. It's part of the process. The aftermath always hits heavy: the fog, the emotional weight, the disconnect from my center. It dulls my spirit, dims my light, and leaves me feeling off. And every time it happens, it makes my commitment to a clearer, more sober life much stronger.

There are a handful of people out there who have seen me drink since I began writing this book. At first, I was incredibly terrified of looking hypocritical. But now I realize my fears only stem from what I perceive as their narrow viewpoint of me and my journey. In general, I've noticed that if people are unable to put you in a box and assign clear labels to you (like "sober" or "not sober"), then they make judgments about you so they can more easily compartmentalize you in their minds. As I've said, everyone's journey is a gray spectrum, not black and white. So, if you experience a similar judgment or criticism, I encourage you to reflect on why it makes you feel insecure. And then **_promptly give less fucks_**.

I was silent about my sobriety for the first three months, and I wish I had shared it with close friends and family sooner. I was so worried people would think I had a bigger problem than it was, and I was especially worried about what co-workers would think. I also wasn't even sure what my journey would look like or how long I would continue staying sober. Again, I was afraid of people compartmentalizing me based on a simple statement like "I stopped drinking." All the initial shame and insecurities are big feelings that are part of the process. At 90 days in, I posted on social media that I was on a sober journey. There's something about posting it online that makes it more real and strengthens your commitment because you want to stay truthful about your post.

The 21/90 rule states that it takes 21 days to make a habit and 90 days to make it a permanent lifestyle change. And energetically, I felt this. An empowering shift happens at 90 days. I felt much more in control, my body felt more stabilized, and I was settling into this new lifestyle.

When I got vocal about my journey, all kinds of people came forward to support me. People I had known for years shared that they were sober for X number of years. People that I partied with that I *thought* were drinking admitted that they only drank very occasionally. I connected with other friends who had stopped drinking around the same time, and we made plans for sober activities. Turns out, the support system I needed was already there— I just had to be real enough to call it in. Vulnerability cracked the door open, and connection walked right through.

My Drunk Resume

So now that you've seen where I'm at, let's rewind. Because before the clarity, before the shift, there was chaos. Welcome to *My Drunk Resume.*

I'm not here to write a full-blown autobiography— just the essentials. Think of this section as a quick-and-dirty overview of the shit I've lived through that makes me qualified to talk about this. Because let's be real, no one wants advice from someone who hasn't been in the trenches.

I started experimenting with "drugs and alcohol" when I was 15. I'm using the term "drugs and alcohol," but I hate that term. It separates alcohol like it's somehow safer or more acceptable— but the truth is, alcohol is a drug too. And honestly, out of everything I've tried, it's been the most damaging one by far.

Around 1999-2000, I discovered rave culture, and it was like stepping into an entirely new universe. Growing up, I always felt like an outsider, never quite finding a group where I truly fit in. I always felt like a weirdo— until I found raves, where the weirdos came together, and suddenly, I wasn't the oddest one in the room. Radical creative self-expression wasn't just accepted; it was celebrated. Judgment was replaced with unconditional acceptance. It was a truly safe space, a world built on the foundation of PLUR— Peace, Love, Unity, and Respect. Dancing at raves became like church to me— a ritual with my chosen community where we would lose ourselves, together, in the flow of the music. It was a space where I could fully exist in the present moment, free from judgment, intuitively moving energy through my body, releasing what no longer served me, and amplifying the collective good vibes of the room. For one night at a time, we existed in a euphoric, almost otherworldly bubble, only to carry that magic with us and scatter it like charged stardust into the rest of the world.

But we all know that along with the rave culture came drugs. I tried alcohol, marijuana, nicotine, MDMA, ketamine, mushrooms, LSD, and cocaine all within about a year. That sounds bad when I write it all out, but none of the drugs I've listed here were as detrimental to me as ALCOHOL. As a person who's done most of the popular drugs in the world (except heroin), alcohol is the most soul-sucking, depressing, and hurtful substance out there, in my opinion. The strange thing is that this is *common knowledge* in America, and most people continue to sweep it under the rug. It's absolute insanity.

Alcohol was normalized in my house growing up, just like most of America, it seems. My dad drank pretty much every day and still does, but he also never missed work. So, when I moved out at 19, got my own place while going to college, and started drinking regularly, it felt like a weird rite of passage. Like, *ah yes, adulthood: bills, hangovers, and showing up anyway.* I was following the family blueprint— drink, function, repeat.

I typically hung out with people a few years older than me, so getting alcohol was never an issue. I'll never forget going to one of my usual bars on my birthday and casually dropping that it was my 21st birthday. The bartenders looked at me like, *"Wait, what?"* They'd been serving me for years, assuming I was legal just because of who I rolled with. It was funny in the moment, but looking back, not exactly as cool as it felt then.

In my adult life, I've lived in Wilmington, NC, Atlanta, GA, and New York City— each with a deeply ingrained drinking culture. While it's unfair to judge these cities as heavy-drinking cities, it was my personal experience. I was operating at a lower frequency, being caught in more negative emotions, and naturally, attracted similar energy and behaviors. After all, that is how the law of attraction works— what you focus on, you bring in.

In my early 20s, Wilmington was where I fully embraced my role as a high-achieving lush. It's where I landed my first tailoring job in the film industry on "One Tree Hill," designed multiple fashion collections, showed at the biggest Fashion Week in the Southeast, and got my work into stores and online. I had studied fashion design with no intention of working in film— until I realized the industry offered high pay, plenty of job opportunities, and at that time suffered a serious lack of talent in the area, making it easy for me to break in. But the reality of the work was far from glamorous— long hours, grueling conditions, and sometimes mind-numbing boredom. It was so monotonous that showing up hungover barely made a difference in my work performance. So, I did. In some twisted way, it even made the soul-sucking nature of the job more tolerable. Back then, I felt like I was living the dream when I could walk (or stumble) home from Wilmington's downtown bars.

In Atlanta, it seemed like everyone I met was at the same level of absolute debauchery. Smoking was even allowed in some top-notch shitty dive bars in East Atlanta and Little Five Points, adding to the chaos. Meanwhile, my career was coming along well. I worked on even bigger projects in the film industry, honing my pattern-making skills and leading entire tailor workshops, such as on the show *Stranger Things*. The hours were longer, the stress was relentless, and my way of coping remained the same— more drinking. A difficult breakup only fueled my habits further.

Toward the end of my time in Atlanta, while working on the show I just mentioned, I experienced a traumatic event during filming where I could have lost my life. Two generators located immediately next to my work trailer were spewing odorless, colorless, but deadly carbon monoxide directly into my workspace via a cooling fan vented from the outside. The resulting hospitalization left me both physically and emotionally destabilized and vulnerable. My stomach was so fucked up from the poison, I could barely eat for a month, and I lost 20 pounds. No one on the crew wanted to acknowledge what had happened because they were so terrified of a lawsuit, and I felt completely abandoned by the crew. Seriously, I gave 12 hours a day for 8 months to this goddamn production and no one could admit that I was placed in a dangerous situation? The easiest way to cope? Drink even more! Sweep it all under the rug— the exhaustion, the abandonment, the physical sickness, the facing my own mortality. And continue working for a soulless industry that almost killed me. Insert a red flag the size of Kansas here.

Within the same month of falling down the stairs and the carbon monoxide poisoning, another breakup from another alcohol-driven relationship spiraled into a full-blown stalker situation. I was terrified in Atlanta, looking over my shoulder all the time, even feeling unsafe in my own house. After catching him trying to break into my home on camera, a restraining order was placed, I packed my shit as fast as I could, and moved to New York City one week later. How did I process all these life-altering events and emotions, you ask? I didn't. I drank.

In New York, the absence of car responsibilities made indulging even easier— any time, any place, with no real barriers. It was a lush's dream, and I fully embraced it.

Because of the lingering mental and physical effects of the carbon monoxide accident, I decided to take an intentional break from the industry to explore other opportunities in New York. I worked as an assistant designer for contemporary dance companies, as a pattern maker for several department store brands, and in what was easily the most enjoyable chapter of my career—creating drag costumes alongside a designer from *Project Runway*. But, as always, the film world found a way to pull me back in. Sewing had taken a toll on my body over the years, and pattern making was mentally draining. These were compounded by the everyday challenges of simply living in New York. Drinking felt essential to unwind, decompress, and make the exhaustion more bearable. As if I needed another reason to drink, COVID hit one year after I moved to NY, and sure enough, the liquor stores stayed open and fully stocked.

The last three years of my time in New York were spent in Bushwick, the most vibrant and exciting neighborhood in Brooklyn. The energy of the streets echoed the rave culture I had always loved— where freedom of expression and unapologetic authenticity were not just accepted, but celebrated. My apartment was just half a block from Maria Hernandez Park, and within a seven-minute walk in any direction, I could find myself at some of the most iconic clubs in the world. I learned to DJ in New York and was able to pick up a few gigs relatively quickly. Although they never paid that much, at least I got drunk for free. I had reached the fucking pinnacle of partying, and sixteen-year-old me was proud. As a stark contrast to my lived experience, I also got mostly sober later while living in this neighborhood.

~ ~ ~

Alcohol was such a "normal" part of my life. It's what I did with friends, after work or school, at dinner, on the beach— basically, it was woven into almost every aspect of my life. On a normal night after work, I'd have maybe three drinks — nothing "crazy." But weekends? Whole different animal. Fridays, I would start the literal second I was off work. Saturdays, I was easily throwing back 8 to 10 drinks, starting earlier, going harder. And Sunday brunch? That was a socially acceptable excuse to keep the weekend buzz rolling, mimosas in hand before noon. So yeah, those are not numbers you wanna scribble down honestly on the "How many drinks per week?" form at the doctor's office. 35-40? Yikes. Every once in a while, I'd take a day or two off to prove to myself that I wasn't *technically* addicted. Spoiler alert: the fact that I even needed to run that little test was the loudest red flag of all.

I've always been kind of an introvert, so I told myself drinking made me "more social," like it unlocked some cooler, looser version of me. But the truth is, I didn't just drink when I was around people — I drank when I was alone, too. And not in some casual, one-glass-of-wine way. I *partied* with myself. Full-blown solo ragers. It wasn't cute. It wasn't quirky. It was me running from myself. Because sitting in silence with my own thoughts? Terrified me. And booze was the fastest way to drown the noise before it could swallow me whole.

I was "really good" at drinking — like, a straight-up professional. For 20 years, I kept my shit together. I maintained high work standards, advanced my skills and career relatively effortlessly, and rarely missed work due to hangovers. I had it dialed in — a fine-tuned system where I knew exactly how much I could drink and still drag myself through the next morning without anyone noticing. But if I'm being real? I never actually *felt* good. My body had just adapted to living in a constant low-grade hangover — a background hum of feeling like trash. My mind? Mushy, gray, heavy as hell. Whatever I drank at night, I'd counterbalance with an equal amount of coffee the next day— not that it helped. I even got all proud of myself for buying "vitamins for drinkers," like that was somehow gonna save me. And I stayed religious about keeping those little bottles stocked, like it was proof I was *taking care* of myself. [Insert eye roll]

Every relationship I had revolved around drinking. I needed a partner in debauchery. Matching my party level wasn't just a preference but a dating requirement, and often the glue of the relationship. I remember talking to someone on a dating app in New York who told me he didn't drink. At the time, when I was drinking heavily, that was an instant dealbreaker. Looking back, his influence could have been exactly what I needed. But the truth is, I wasn't ready to cut back until I decided for myself.

There's no other drug that hijacks your soul the way alcohol does. Have you ever looked into someone's eyes when they're drunk and realized they're not there anymore? They're not looking *at* you, they're looking *through* you with those hazed, empty, drunken eyes. You know deep down that whatever comes out of their mouth next isn't *them* talking. It's something darker. Meaner. Hollow. Some fucked-up ghost puppeteering their body while you're stuck there, trying to clean up the wreckage — dragging them home, praying they don't hurt themselves or anyone else in the process. I'd love to say I've never been that person. But here's the thing: when you're that far gone, you don't remember. And maybe that's the most terrifying part.

Dark Night

The "Dark Night of the Soul" isn't just a bad day, a breakup, or a rough patch you cry your way through. It's a full-scale annihilation of everything you thought you knew about yourself, your life, your purpose. It's standing naked in the ruins of your old identity with no fucking map, no safety net, and no way to numb the pain. It's the kind of spiritual unraveling that strips you down to nothing so that something real can finally be born. I didn't know the name for what I was going through at first — not until I was about eight months sober and already neck-deep in it — but once I heard the words *Dark Night of the Soul,* it hit me like a truth I'd been living without even realizing it. This chapter is the story of that darkness — the void, the letting go, the wild trust it took to surrender, and how losing everything I thought I needed gave me a kind of freedom I didn't even know existed.

After making a pilgrimage to Burning Man, that annual week-long, no-holds-barred desert celebration of art, music, self-expression, and community, I came back to a world that no longer made sense. I was cracked wide open. Burning Man didn't just shake up my reality — it shattered it, forcing me to see everything through a completely new lens. It was like the universe hit the reset button, stripping away everything fake and showing me the raw, unfiltered truth of who I really was.

I felt existentially homeless, like I didn't belong anywhere—homesick for a place I couldn't remember. It was like I was spiraling into a black hole, no gravity to hold me, just floating in this infinite void with nothing to hold on to. The outside world seemed to trigger me at every turn, amplifying the traumas within me that were crying out to be healed.

Everything I once believed to be true no longer made sense. The spiritual teachers I had turned to for guidance no longer made any fucking sense — just empty words now. And in that moment of disillusionment, something shifted. It was a fascinating discovery. With everyone else's guidance no longer resonating, I had no choice but to turn inward. I was forced to find my center, to trust myself. And that's when I had the most powerful realization: everything they had been preaching was already inside of me. I didn't need them to find the truth. I was the truth.

I felt that I could see right through everyone's bullshit and ended up cutting people out of my life— some temporarily (even my own mother) and some permanently.

Sobriety made me painfully aware of how much I'd let myself be walked on— no boundaries, no self-respect. And when I started standing up for myself, that's when people started falling away. They didn't want the version of me that was waking up. They wanted the doormat, the overly nice, over-accommodating version of Casey— the drunk version.

I detached from everything so much, it felt like I had nothing left. No people, no beliefs, no foundation. But with all that loss, there was a strange kind of freedom. I had no choice but to let the empty space in. I surrendered to the darkness, even leaned into it, trusting that the void would fill with things that were real— things aligned with the true me.

I felt more alone than ever. But for the first time, it felt like a necessary kind of solitude. Surrendering became this wild practice— terrifying, yes, but also magical. I realized that all the answers I needed were already within me. In that moment, something inside me cracked wide open, and a cosmic explosion of power began.

The ripple effect from that implosion? It made me fucking fearless, because I learned to not be afraid of *nothing,* itself.

Having nothing is the key to freedom.

Through surrendering to the dark, the seedlings of this book began to sprout, and sharing my darkness felt like the only way back to the light.

The Spiritual Effects of Alcohol

I've always been highly sensitive and spiritually attuned from a young age. I drank for a large part of my life, and there's no doubt I grew spiritually and learned a ton of lessons as a highly functioning lush. But when I stopped drinking, that spiritual connection *skyrocketed*. The contrast of the spiritual journey with and without alcohol is like night and day. The clarity, depth, and connection I experience now daily are incomparable. I love being more connected to elevated emotions and more in tune with the beautiful nuances of life, and for me, this is a huge motivating factor to stay sober.

Think about some of the reasons you drink, off the top of your head. Is it confidence, soothing the nervous system, a desire for connection/vulnerability, a desire to express yourself authentically and speak your truth, or a desire to reach an altered state? ***These reasons are our sources of*** *conditioning and areas of potential soul growth.* When we drink, we in a way *borrow* these energies from alcohol. We borrow confidence, borrow vulnerability, borrow relaxation. But borrowing comes with a cost— not just physical, but energetic hangovers as well. Emotional debt. *Delaying* the natural growth of your soul. Because with regular use, we are teaching our bodies that it needs a substance to feel safe or expressive. Not working through uncomfortable situations for the purpose of our souls' learning to evolve.

I drank for all the reasons listed above, but one in particular stands out in this chapter. I had a desire to reach an altered state. A more connected, in-tune state. To try to remember my own true energy by attempting to push aside the density and heaviness of planet Earth with the use of alcohol. The desire to be **IN THE NOW,** not worried about past mistakes or future problems. Because the present moment is our greatest connection to Source. But instead of deepening my spiritual connection, alcohol only amplified the disconnect. After learning to connect without a crutch, it now feels as though life itself is an altered state.

~ ~ ~

I have survived three highly unusual and life-threatening traumatic incidents— any one of which could have ended my life. Instead of fully processing these experiences, I drank my way through them, numbing the impact and delaying the healing. Had I faced these events without alcohol, I would have been able to work through the emotions in real time rather than

42

pushing them aside with the poison. Sobriety doesn't erase trauma, but it does allow space for true healing.

As a result, much of the healing required to recover from these traumas (and many others) had been buried beneath years of avoidance. When I got mostly sober, all of it resurfaced. This is exactly why quitting drinking can feel so overwhelmingly difficult— it's not just about giving up alcohol, it's about facing everything we tried to numb. The emotions, the pain, the unresolved wounds— they don't disappear just because we ignored them. They patiently wait for us, demanding to be acknowledged and healed the moment we stop drowning them out.

~~~

Alcohol lowers our frequency. Think of our bodies on Earth as antennas, constantly transmitting and receiving energy. These antennas connect us from the physical world to the astral plane, broadcasting our vibrational frequency wherever we go. When we are ungrounded (a state that we go to when we are drunk or hungover) and disconnected from the Earth's energy, our antennas can't reach very high, keeping us stuck in lower vibrational states— and trapped in emotional loops of shame, guilt, fear, and anger. However, when we are deeply rooted, energetically aligned, authentic, and in sync with the Earth's natural rhythms, our antennas extend higher, allowing us to access elevated states of consciousness, such as love, joy, and peace, which result from a deep connection to source energy. The more grounded we are, the more expansive our frequency becomes, creating a bridge between the physical and the divine.

Our antennas emit a unique frequency, allowing us to tune into people, places, and experiences that match our energetic state. Alcohol acts like a heavy fog, a dense veil that distorts and dulls our signal. It blocks our ability to connect with higher frequencies and keeps us stuck in a lower vibrational state. When I look back at the times in my life when I drank the heaviest, I see with absolute clarity how my low vibration pulled in other low-vibrational people, thoughts, and situations. It was a magnet for chaos, a feedback loop of fear, apathy, shame, and judgment— sometimes even a full-on downward spiral.

Take a moment to reflect on this law of attraction— what have you attracted into your life when your frequency was high? Now, compare that to what showed up when your frequency was low. The difference is undeniable.

~~~

When we remove alcohol, we remove the interference. Our frequency clears, our intuition strengthens, and we begin attracting a reality that aligns with our highest good.

When I stopped drinking, it was as if a dark cloud had finally lifted. But with light comes shadows. And what a gift that is! I couldn't see my own shadows (or trauma) when I was surrounded by darkness— when they blended into the dark chaos of my old reality. But now, with clarity in the light, they stand out in sharp contrast, allowing me to truly see them, acknowledge them, comfort them, and let them know they are safe to be seen and released.

One by one, I'm shining light on my shadows, peeling back the layers of what alcohol kept hidden for so long. I've had incredibly low self-esteem my entire life, something that has been constant work to raise, and I used to drink to fake being confident. When I stopped, I allowed myself to sit with this feeling and examine it.

Growing up, I wanted nothing more than to be friends with my older brother (who is three years older than I). He did what probably any older sibling did to their younger sibling: "No, you're not cool enough to hang out," "girls are gross," "you're dumb," etc. The rejection and belittling happened so often that it got ingrained in my brain that I wasn't good enough. I don't hold it against him; we were just kids and innocent victims of the trash TV we were fed in the early 90s. This feeling of *not being good enough* was a subconscious motivator in my life, fueling high motivation over-achievement, which wasn't the worst trickle-down effect. But that low self-esteem carried over into my romantic relationships when I started dating. I went for the first guy who gave me attention and had almost zero actual standards of my own. And in combination with drinking often, it made for some pretty awful relationships where I bent over backwards for the smallest amount of validation.

When I got sober and realized this was happening, I was able to release the need for validation from my brother. When I released the need to be *liked* by him, and truly started giving less fucks, I wrote him a letter, bringing all of this to his attention. Why was I *protecting him* from knowing he caused me trauma in the first place? He was oblivious to the depth he had affected me with his negative words, but it felt good to lay it all out on the table. There is so much healing in simple acknowledgement.

So, when I say peeling back the layers of healing, I mean it. You may not even realize yet the levels of connection something has, but it's so exciting when the dots get connected. A seemingly simple self-reflection of low self-esteem turned into not only feeling more confident by *releasing the need for validation* and *not needing to prove myself*, but also *healing my relationship* with my brother, and then *recognizing and breaking my negative relationship patterns* in order to move forward with healthier romantic relationships. Holy shit!

~ ~ ~

Guidance from source energy or your higher self is more difficult to attain when alcohol is involved. Connection will only be granted when your vessel is pure enough for higher vibrational energy to enter. This is not an overnight process— it's an ongoing lifestyle change.

Hate to be the bearer of obvious news here, but things that you know are good for you, guess what— raise your vibration! The things I'm about to say here are going to sound like some typical "love and light" spiritual advice, but maybe someone needs to hear it. If you want to work on raising your vibration, incorporate these things into your life on a regular basis, in addition to cutting out alcohol:

- Eat clean, organic, unprocessed foods, limit sugar
- Get plenty of sunshine and connection to nature (you can even literally connect to the earth, a practice called grounding)

- Move your body mindfully in ways you like (Dance? Yoga?)
- Create art. Just create.
- Laugh. Laugh so hard it hurts.
- Breathwork
- Meditation
- Work with crystals
- Practice gratitude
- Work with sound vibrations (Hertz frequencies, solfeggio tones, binaural beats, live healing instruments)
- Authentic expression (speaking your truth)

~ ~ ~

In addition to lowering our vibration and keeping us stuck in unhealed trauma loops, alcohol disconnects us from our authenticity. According to the Scale of Positive and Negative Experiences (SPANE) scale, it is suggested that authenticity vibrates higher than love or gratitude. So, when the bottle is doing the talking and your soul is just watching, we lose our authenticity because our actions are being induced by the *alcohol,* not our true selves. One of the biggest lessons we are all here to learn on this soul bootcamp is learning how to come home to ourselves. To remember who you were before the world told you who to be. And I'll be honest— if you're ready to answer the call, alcohol isn't part of the mission.

Without that alcoholic cloud distorting my signal, lowering my vibration, and disconnecting me from my true self, my antenna reaches higher, tuning into those higher frequencies more and more often. I am more in love with life by living authentically, more at peace, and more thankful. A headspace I never could have imagined when I was in the alcohol trap. As I became more in tune with myself, I noticed that I began attracting people and situations that aligned with my energy. The more I embraced that shift, the more positive things started coming back to me in ways I couldn't have predicted. Riding those high-frequency waves feels like an exciting game to me now— genuinely curious and excited for what the future holds. What once felt like wrestling with the universe every damn day now feels more like a cosmic prank I'm finally learning to laugh at.

Part 2: A Removed Point of View

Why Do We Drink?

Isn't it ironic that a common reason why we drink is often the same reason we turn to books like this— *a desire to end our suffering?*

Alcohol acceptance is ingrained in us from a young age, weaving its influence through various channels such as advertising, film, television, social scenarios, and even workplace settings. From catchy commercials depicting glamorous social scenes to the normalization of drinking in everyday social interactions, the message is clear: in our society, alcohol consumption is not only acceptable but openly *encouraged.*

It's no wonder alcohol has such a grip on us— it's the most widely consumed addictive drug in the United States. It's everywhere. It's normalized, glamorized, and pumped into our culture with billions of dollars behind it. Drinking isn't just accepted, it's expected. It's sold to us as the key to connection, relaxation, and celebration. Saying no to alcohol in a world built around it can feel like trying to swim upstream in a river determined to pull you under.

But if you're reading this, you've already begun to turn around in that current. Maybe you're tired. Maybe you're curious. Maybe you're quietly wondering, *Why do I actually drink?* Whatever brought you here, let this be a moment of recognition: you're stronger than you think. And you're not alone in asking these questions.

For a long time, I didn't know why I drank either. I just did— almost every day. I told myself it was social, creative, and fun— but if I'm honest, it was a way to keep my feelings and sensitivity at bay. I rarely allowed myself to experience my emotions fully. Instead, I cycled between numbing out and recovering from it, always on autopilot. I never gave myself enough time or space without alcohol to explore the deeper reasons behind my constant desire to drink.

I had no idea that my emotional patterns were stuck in a feedback loop— like my lifelong lean toward pessimism and my discomfort with feeling my feelings— were silently guiding my drinking and keeping me trapped in those lower vibration emotions.

If you're anything like me, you're a certain kind of eccentric — too emotionally rebellious to ever fully blend into "normal" society. We're the creatives, the free spirits, the empaths who feel everything a little too deeply. We see how broken the world is, and even though we dream of making it better, we often feel powerless against its weight. We carry sadness that isn't always ours. Living on the fringe of society feels more at home. We find mainstream life tedious and uninspiring, craving variety, meaning, and the strange beauty that hides in the cracks. Our curious minds chase the extraordinary, drawn to experiences that color outside the lines, including mind-altering substances. Maybe those substances gave us a brief escape— a way to forget the pain, the loneliness, the constant feeling of being different. We're also stubborn as hell— strong-willed, determined, relentless when we set our sights on something. It's a superpower when channeled into the right dreams. Except when the goal becomes *"I'm going to get fucked up tonight."*

The good news is: that sensitivity? That stubbornness? That emotional depth? It's not your weakness—it's your raw material. Once you turn inward with honesty and compassion, those same traits become the fire behind your healing.

During the process of getting mostly sober, I dove deep into various spiritual teachings and concepts that helped me unravel why I drank— and more importantly, *why* I am the way I am. When we understand our personal "Whys?" it allows us to move through life with greater compassion and clarity toward ourselves.

And now, I hope you do the same. As you move through this book, I invite you to stay open— to your truth, your questions, your strength. You don't have to have it all figured out. You just have to be willing to look. Because the more you understand about yourself, the easier it becomes to let go of what no longer serves you.

Freedom begins with awareness. You are worthy of that freedom.

Acknowledging the Craving

You're not broken and you're not weak for having alcohol cravings. If you've ever felt stuck in a craving spiral, confused about where it's coming from or why it hits so hard, you're not alone, and you're not crazy. There's nothing wrong with you. Cravings don't make you flawed; they're messengers. They show up to teach, not to punish. This chapter is about learning how to listen from a different perspective— a higher place.

Most of us are so used to reacting to a craving that we barely notice when we shift into autopilot, and suddenly we're pouring a drink. But something magical happens when we pause, step back, and observe our thoughts and cravings instead of getting swept up in them. That's what this chapter is about: waking up to your *observer self*— the version of you that can sit with discomfort without being ruled by it.

Here, we explore what it means to operate from a higher mind perspective— a way to stay grounded when old patterns flare up. We'll talk about how to recognize cravings for what they are (clues, not commands), how to listen for the wisdom underneath them, and how to gently, powerfully shift your response.

Because the truth is, you're already powerful. You've always had this calm, steady part of you, your higher self, that knows how to guide you home. This chapter helps you reconnect with that part. You don't need to force it. You just need to remember it's there.

A Higher Mind Perspective

Imagine sitting on a park bench on a beautiful day, entirely at peace. You experience a calm, inner stillness that enables you to embrace the present moment fully. This stillness is your true essence— your higher self. The warm sun kisses your skin, and your eyes take in the simple yet stunning view of lush green grass and trees swaying gently in the breeze.

Then, an alcohol craving strolls by. Perhaps it's accompanied by Sadness, tagging along like an uninvited guest. You begin to feel uneasy. You slump down, making yourself small, and hope they don't notice you sitting there. Too late: you've already spotted each other. But here's the thing—*you don't have to interact with Craving or with Sadness.* You can remain on your bench, smiling, and simply observe these two seemingly inseparable best friends. Take a moment to notice Sadness. What does it look like? Does it have a color, a shape, or even a face? Does someone specific come to mind? Where do you feel it in your body? If you're curious, you might choose to have a conversation with Sadness to understand why it's visiting today. *But remember, you don't have to get emotionally entangled in the drama.* You're in control, rooted in your calm and unshakable stillness. Sadness and Craving will get bored, shrug, and walk away soon enough when you don't give them a seat at the table or offer them comfy chairs— and a drink.

The simple act of acknowledging our alcohol cravings puts us in a position to move through them more easily. Let's first recognize the separation between our higher selves and our earthly selves. I was first introduced to the concept of observing my thoughts from a higher mind perspective through Eckhart Tolle's book *The Power of Now*, in which he explains the idea that you are not your mind. I highly recommend this book if this concept is new to you.

Our higher self— whether we call it spirit, soul, or essence— is our true nature. It's the little voice who truly does KNOW— the one who whispers to you but very rarely screams. That one in the back of your mind that quietly says, "This might not be the best idea," to which we often reply, *"Shut up, I'm having fun!"* When we quiet our obsessive busyness and encourage our reactionary lower minds to settle down, we can learn to 'flip the switch' and observe our thoughts and bodies from a higher-self perspective, activating a fantastic internal guidance system. The resulting clarity, detachment, and wisdom that can flow to you when this channel is opened is a gift that is yours 24/7— a gift you've always had, and like a muscle, it's a gift that grows stronger the more it is used. This concept aligns with some meditation practices for those who want to explore it further, but embracing this perspective doesn't require formal meditation or training—it's a perspective shift accessible to all of us when we're ready.

Operating from this observational standpoint gives us power, which you can utilize in your daily life. By observing the craving and the emotions attached to it, we can decide how they need to be acknowledged in that moment. Sometimes, muffled emotions may arise— ones we've already worked through and processed—and they don't need to take hold of us. Other times, the emotions are strong, new, raw, and fresh, like an open wound that requires gentle care. Tips for working through these emotions can be found later in the *Craving Scenarios* and *Support Tools* sections.

When I have given in to an alcohol craving, it's usually been an unconscious act driven by a state of disconnection. In those moments, I'm disconnected from my higher self, allowing my emotions or my reactive lower mind to dictate my actions, and I have given in to drinking as an old habit without mindful consideration as to what I'm doing. Bored? Go for a walk and surprise— the muscle memory of my feet took me right to the wine store! Anxious or awkward at a party? My subconscious strategically positions me next to the cooler so I can grab another when I finish the first. It's wild to notice the reactionary way we are used to consuming.

Noticing it happening is a necessary step in breaking the pattern. Watch yourself, as if you're watching your own movie, and confront the craving head-on. By consciously acknowledging the moments we want to drink, we give ourselves the power to consciously choose a different response instead of automatically reaching for a drink. The real, life-changing work starts when we understand the deeper reasons behind each craving to drink and choose how we want to respond.

Say it Out Loud

This may seem counterintuitive or vulnerable as hell, but if you have a craving, *tell someone about it.* They're not secrets anymore— we have to acknowledge their existence if we ever wish to be free of them. Have a safe support system in place: a partner, friend, family member, therapist, dry buddy, sober in-person or online community, or a journal. At first, it may seem to you that if you acknowledge it, it will just grow stronger and soon you'll have no choice but to give in. Oddly, it's the opposite that happens. The simple act of expressing your craving will take its power away more quickly, just like letting an emotion move through you instead of suppressing it. The power to make a conscious choice rather than a reactive one returns to you. You're the boss!

Get to the Bottom of the Craving

Every craving comes from a need. Simple as that. You're not weak, you're not a mess— you're a human being with real, valid needs. And ignoring those needs or shaming yourself for having them? That's what keeps the cycle going. Maybe you just want to feel like you belong at the party. Maybe you're trying to fill this aching emptiness you can't quite name. Maybe you're avoiding something hard, painful, or boring as hell. Whatever it is, it deserves your attention, not your judgment.

The power comes back to you when you stop numbing and start getting curious. When you ask: *What do I really need right now?* And then actually listen. That's how cravings lose their grip. That's how you stop reaching for the drink and start reaching for what you *actually* need. Being "needy" isn't a flaw. It's human. It's honest. And when you start meeting those needs with care instead of avoidance, that's when everything starts to shift.

Cravings don't just show up out of nowhere. There's always a reason— and the more willing you are to dig into what's really going on underneath, the faster they lose their power. It's not about controlling the craving. It's about understanding it. Start asking questions. Be brutally honest with yourself. Get curious instead of critical. This is where the real work lives.

Journaling can be a total game-changer here. Not the pretty, filtered kind— just you, pen, paper, and the truth. Let it pour out. Let it be messy. Let it be real. That's how you get to the root of what's driving the craving— and that's how you start to change it for good.

I've written some questions to get you started when the urge hits. If you'd like to dive deeper, refer to *Support Tool 2: Craving Journal Prompts*.

Part 3: Craving Scenarios

Quitting alcohol is fucking hard. Let's not sugarcoat it. Cravings can sneak up on you from every direction— when you're sad, pissed off, overwhelmed, even when you're happy or celebrating. It's wild how your brain will try to convince you that a drink solves *everything*.

In this section, I'm gonna get personal. I'll walk you through some of my own cravings— what triggered them, how I handled them (or didn't), and what I learned through the messy, nonlinear process of slowly reprogramming my mind and body to stop reaching for the bottle on autopilot.

When I got mostly sober, I dove deep into spiritual work— not to become some saint, but to finally get to the root of my shit. I needed to understand *why* I kept reaching for alcohol, *why* I felt so uncomfortable in my own skin, and *why* numbing out felt safer than being fully alive.

That's what this chapter— and honestly, this whole book— is about. It's about uncovering your deeper "why" so you can stop running and start healing. And once you start breaking free from these unconscious patterns, you'll feel it, not just in your sobriety, but in every part of your life. It's lighter. It's freer. It's more real.

Some of these Scenarios begin by setting the scene in italics. I invite you to journey into the moment of the craving alongside me so that we may break it down from the inside out.

You ready? Let's go.

Craving Scenario: I'm Fucking Bored

I'm feeling fine... coasting on neutral ground. Then it hits—around 6 or 7 p.m., I want alcohol. This is the time of day I've had my first drink of the day for years. It makes me wonder—what did I even do with all those evenings? The last time I remember being bored was as a kid. So why now? It's such an unfamiliar feeling— what the hell do I DO?

It's nearly impossible to feel bored when you're drunk. Boredom was one of the main reasons I first tried alcohol as a teenager. I grew up in Burlington, North Carolina, a small town in the middle of the state. I was a very creative child— had to be able to combat boredom. Then came alcohol— a quick and easy escape. Suddenly, I didn't need to use my brain or get up and do something to fill the void. Drinking numbed the boredom and created a sense of false fun. It was so much easier.

Quitting drinking can feel incredibly boring at first— there's no denying it. When alcohol has been a primary source of dopamine rewards, adjusting to life without it requires patience. As your brain recalibrates to its natural dopamine levels, the absence of those artificial highs can make everything feel dull by comparison (More on this in *Craving Scenario: I Just Want to Fucking Party*). But it won't stay this way forever. Stick with it, and over time, you'll rediscover joy in life's simple pleasures. It's not always obvious at first that what you're feeling *isn't* emptiness— it's just... stillness. And that stillness can be beautiful once you stop running from it.

"Addiction is a progressive narrowing of the things that bring you pleasure. Happiness is a progressive expansion of the things that bring you pleasure. The former emerges passively. The latter takes work."

– Andrew D. Huberman, Ph.D.

Boredom is inherently a *void*, and like most things, it can be interpreted positively, negatively, or neutrally. It becomes a negative void when it leads to self-judgment— am I craving a drink because I feel uninteresting or lack hobbies? If so, it's time to unpack that. Any negative emotions that arise from boredom offer a valuable opportunity— a gift to acknowledge, process, and release them, paving the way to move forward in a healthier and more balanced way. In turn, what initially felt negative can transform into something with a positive purpose.

Perhaps the boredom stems from societal pressure to stay constantly busy? What if I embraced the peace of doing nothing instead of incessantly filling my time? Mastering the art of doing nothing— without boredom or the nagging feeling that it's wrong— is a form of rebellion. It frees us from both internal and external pressures and deserves a gold star in my book.

I prefer to look at boredom as a positive portal into new possibilities. That sounds like a fuckin Mary Poppins quote or something, but I'm going with it. It creates space for fresh ideas, creativity, and insights you might never have discovered while drinking.

~ ~ ~

Think about when we were kids. Out of boredom, we came up with the most fun games or activities to do with our friends. In contrast, passing out on the couch at home alone isn't fun or interesting. It simply numbs us enough that we no longer care about what was done with that time, or leaves us unable to remember it at all. Did you just need to give yourself permission to do nothing?

It's time to create a life we don't need to escape from or feel bored by. This isn't a quick fix— it's an ongoing process. Many of us have used alcohol to enhance mundane experiences, but real life doesn't work that way. Looking back, it's cringeworthy to think of how much time I wasted sitting around, doing absolutely nothing in dark bars or at home. It only felt like fun because I was drunk.

So, what do we do with our time? I found this quote that was incredibly helpful for me in the first year of sobriety (and even now) when I was wandering through life trying to find my way:

"Act on your excitement, in that moment, at every moment."

—Bashar channeling

The "excitement" they speak of does not have to be dopamine-releasing level excitement. Tune into the little nudges your soul is telling you. Capture those twinges of excitement and act on them. Sometimes, the most exciting thing I can do is be in my bed with little to no stimulation, and I will 100% honor that that is what my soul needs to heal at that time.

In early sobriety, I had an "A-ha!" moment when I realized I was experiencing PEACE, not boredom. We are so used to the exaggerated dopamine ups and downs that alcohol brings that a steady, lovely feeling of peacefully doing very little can be confused with boredom. Recognize and appreciate.

For a deeper perspective on boredom, we must also consider the low attention span and ADD culture we live in. If our brains are constantly trained for the quick, dopamine-driven hits from platforms like Instagram and TikTok, it's no wonder that reading a book or sitting down to do an art project might feel boring at first. This is just another layer to the complexity of boredom. The key point is that giving ourselves time and space to explore what truly excites us might seem boring at first, but it's essential to sit with that feeling to discover what emerges.

"All men's miseries arise from not being able to sit alone in a quiet room." – Blaise Pascal

~ ~ ~

It's truly remarkable how much time seems to open up when you stop drinking. Time feels different— days seem to stretch on, almost twice as long. I really had to stretch my mind to find ways to fill this newfound space. I had to do something, anything, with all this newfound time. A common go-to alcohol replacement is exercise. While I hate most forms, yoga has been the one consistent practice in my life since I was 15. In the beginning, I would often book late classes, knowing that evening cravings would hit every day, and that was the timeframe when I felt the most lost.

For quicker onsets of boredom, I would take a walk, find a fun non-alcoholic drink at my local fancy bodega, start an art project, make it an intentional movie night, cook, read a book, connect with a friend, clean my apartment, deep clean or organization, take online courses, listen to podcasts, write, and the list goes on.

Sometimes, you must take your mind off the craving by intentionally acting to distract, even if you're unmotivated. DO SOMETHING other than drink. Anything else at all; in the end, the only thing that matters in the beginning is that you don't drink. This is your *only* job in the very beginning.

But at the same time, if you can't stop thinking about it, then lean into it through education, banter, or support. Please refer to *Support Tool 1* for podcasts, books, and group recommendations that got me through times like these!

~~~

I started working on mosaic plant pot projects during the COVID-19 pandemic. It was a fun, semi-mindless activity I could do with my hands while drinking. It didn't require much skill, attention, or deep thought. Turns out, it was way more fun while NOT drinking and a thing that could keep me just occupied enough to take my mind off a craving for a drink.

My medium of choice was a broken mirror that I found on the street in Brooklyn. Free and shiny. When I found another broken mirror, it felt like I won the lottery. I found a cheap Styrofoam ball at the miraculous 99 Cent Plus Variety Store on my block. As a party girl at heart, I love disco balls, so I had the idea to make a broken mirror disco ball. One day, I found myself excited to be working on my broken mirror disco ball on a Saturday night, sober, sipping a cherry ginger mocktail I had concocted that had the perfect level of tartness and spice to keep my taste buds interested. In that moment, I reflected (literally in broken glass) on how far I had come. How, 6 months ago, I would have been under a disco ball at some nightclub in my neighborhood, probably about six drinks deep by that time of the night (which wasn't even that late). I was putting together broken pieces of this "puzzle" that was only a puzzle if I decided I wanted it to be a puzzle. I was taking literal trash that was destined never to be seen again and making it into something beautiful. Giving it a second life, giving it a chance to be seen. It felt like I was putting pieces of my soul back together. It felt like a win when an odd shape would fit perfectly into the pieces beside it. Some parts didn't fit quite right, but it didn't matter when the grout filled the gaps and made something beautiful. This project turned out to be incredibly symbolic of my mostly sober journey.

Craving Scenario: Work Sucks

I just worked a 10-hour day and want a drink, like immediately. But why? To unwind, relax my body, and turn off my mind? It seems like a straightforward need, but I'm gonna break it down to be sure...

I used to look forward to and savor that after-work drink, indulging in it almost daily. When I first stopped giving in to that daily craving and began learning about what alcohol does to the body, I discovered that alcohol spikes blood sugar. Was my body partly craving the physical spike I had been giving it around the same time every day?

I realized that on a typical workday, when lunch was around 12 or 1 and I didn't get home until 7, I was starving. Reaching for a drink in those moments would 1) hit me faster on an empty stomach and 2) give me a quick calorie and energy spike to compensate for not eating.

I've noticed that managing my blood sugar levels significantly reduces cravings. I prefer eating small, frequent meals, but I sometimes get so caught up in work that I forget to eat. Now, I make a point to snack in the late afternoon and eat as soon as I get home. It's amazing how much clearer and more rational I feel when my blood sugar is stable.

Another underlying need behind this craving is the desire to relax my body physically. Many of my jobs involve sewing, which can take a toll on my body over time. Sometimes, without realizing it, I carry tension in my body throughout the day, especially when under pressure. After addressing my blood sugar, I prioritize doing something kind for my physical body. This might include stretching, yin yoga, an Epsom salt bath, a foot soak, using a Thera Cane or a massager, or practicing cupping. If I haven't gotten enough movement during the day, the excess stress might need to be released through more vigorous exercise (see more tips in *Craving Scenario: I Feel Anxious*). During my last job, I incorporated exercise into my day by biking to and from work.

Fridays are the toughest for me. This craving often overlaps with the *Let's Celebrate! Craving Scenario*, where the urge for an after-work drink is tied to a sense of accomplishment after surviving another week. When I'm on a regular workweek schedule, I've noticed that how I spend Friday night sets the tone for the entire weekend. Now that I'm not reaching for a drink immediately upon getting off work, waking up with a hangover Saturday, drinking it off, and continuing the cycle Sunday (insert eye roll), I like to set myself up for a healthy weekend if I'm not dead tired. I love grocery shopping and doing a few chores on Friday night to maximize my fun time on Saturday and Sunday. I use that fresh new weekend energy and buy myself flowers instead of a drink, healthy food to make myself brunch in the morning, and/or a special meal over the weekend. A healthy dose of self-love on a Friday night helps to keep me on track for the rest of the weekend. I'm flipping the script from self-destruction to self-care.

The next possible underlying need for the after-work craving is much harder to admit and fix: you hate your job and need to dissociate from not just the day but also the larger undesirable situation you find yourself in.

This can change for me daily, even within the same job and working the same hours. Some days, I absolutely love it— I'm in the flow, feeling energized and stimulated. I come home feeling fulfilled, and after eating, I don't experience any cravings. The urge to drink dissipates when I'm genuinely passionate about what I'm doing.

On other days, I can feel completely drained, whether from being overworked or from feeling under-stimulated and unfulfilled. I hate to break it to you, but if you're feeling this way more often than not, you have a choice: change your situation or change your attitude. Everything else is nonsense.

"The reason we are all so miserable may be because we are working so hard to avoid being miserable."

– Dr. Anna Lembke

Sometimes, the sheer number of hours worked triggers the craving. After about 4-6 hours of focus on a demanding or complex job, I feel maxed out. However, when our capitalistic society has imposed standards of 8+ hour workdays, we often feel ashamed that we are tired after just 5 hours. I'm inviting you to break that unrealistic expectation society has imposed on us. When working for myself, I aim for this ideal daily limit to avoid feeling overworked and tempted to reach for a drink at the end of the day. If you have any flexibility to cut back on your work hours, and this resonates with you, consider experimenting with a reduced schedule. Use the extra time to prioritize self-care and see how it impacts your overall well-being.

I understand that many jobs don't allow for shorter workdays. In that case (and some boss somewhere may hate me for saying this), **do less at your job**. Incorporate self-care into your workday. Take an extra walk, extend your lunch by 5-10 minutes, make that social phone call, or step out as if you're a smoker for a few 10-minute breaks. Slow down— work at a normal pace instead of the top speed you're used to. Take a moment to appreciate a beautiful cup of tea or enjoy the view from a window. Most likely, no one will notice, except perhaps when they see your attitude improving because you're taking better care of yourself. For more on protecting your energy and nurturing yourself, explore *Craving Scenario: It's All Too Much, I Wish I Wasn't So Sensitive,* where I dive into emotional self-care.

During the final stretch of my most recent six-month film job, I started playing positive morning affirmations daily for the last three months. Sometimes, it helped— just a little. But eventually, it became clear that if something fundamental needs to change, you can't fake your way through it anymore. If your job doesn't excite or inspire you in any way, think about the energy you're carrying with you throughout the day and projecting into the world. You might unintentionally become the dark cloud in the room, and that negativity can ripple outward, affecting those around you in ways you may not even realize. It's a domino effect that goes beyond what we can perceive. So, please pay attention to what's weighing you down and take steps to address it, not just for yourself but for the energy you bring to those around you.

When is enough *enough* for you? Use those cravings as a source of information and fuel for change.

~ ~ ~

I've worked freelance my entire life, never having a regular 9-to-5 job. Honestly, I always believed that kind of structure would crush my soul— and thankfully, I've known that about myself for as long as I can remember. Through my freelance adventures, I've experienced the full spectrum of income. I've gone from earning the highest IATSE rates in the country on film gigs in New York, with even higher pay on special shoots, to being completely jobless for months, scraping by on odd jobs friends threw my way. So, let's take a closer look at this spectrum and what it reveals.

When you work more, you often spend more, usually on things you don't need, as a way to compensate for the toll it takes on your soul. During long film job days, I spend money on "self-care," not because I simply deserve it, but because I absolutely *need* it. My body hurts, so massages, saunas, hot yoga classes, or even chiropractor visits become necessities. With no time to cook, I spend more on eating out. To counteract the sadness or stress from work, I buy expensive clothes or other things I don't need, which gives me a fleeting sense of happiness. Once the job is over, I often need time off to recover, which leads to spending more on a vacation to decompress. By the time I'm ready to return to work, I'm back at square one, repeating the cycle. And let's not forget relationships— they're nearly impossible to maintain because there's simply no time or energy left to give.

When I work less, I naturally find ways to be more frugal because I have the time to do so. I can prioritize self-care (or maybe just my basic human needs that shouldn't be labeled as something fancy like "self-care"), which significantly improves my mental health. I have the time to be creative and make clothes that truly make me feel good. I have time to cook nourishing meals, leaving me feeling healthier overall. I can invest in meaningful relationships with friends and family, deepening those connections. The after-work drink craving almost disappears because I feel more balanced and whole as a person.

The after-work drink may stem from a simple physical need, but the deeper psychological needs are often more challenging to face. Creating a work environment that doesn't require a daily drink may also involve social deconditioning— questioning what we "should" be doing for work or what a "normal" work week looks like for our own specific life and needs. Acknowledging what needs to change is a crucial first step in this process.

~ ~ ~

I thought I was born to make clothes. The talent is in my blood, with several close family members having partial or full careers in clothing production. The talent came naturally since the age of 11, and high-level work fell into my lap almost right out of college. It's one of the few areas where I've felt consistent confidence. Millions of people have seen my creations on TV, in movies, and on stages. Some of those projects have been *Stranger Things,* Tim Burton's *Alice in Wonderland, Guardians of the Galaxy,* and *Drag Race.*

But since becoming mostly sober, making clothes that help the rich and famous to become richer and more famous has become trivial, completely unfulfilling, and boring (trigger craving!). I feel I'm not helping enough people and that my skills could potentially be used to fulfill a greater purpose. Feeling stuck in a tailor shop by myself with little human interaction isn't working for me anymore. Although I still love the creative aspects of creating clothing, sometimes the creative opportunities are few and far between, making me feel like a one-person factory.

When I was drinking, I was okay with it because I was on autopilot-robot mode. My days felt unsatisfying, repetitive, or dull, and drinking was an escape. It numbed me to monotony, and I didn't mind the hangovers because it distracted me from how unfulfilled I was. I didn't mind working alone because less human contact while hungover was a bonus back then. And the drinking cycle continued. Now I need something more fulfilling to my soul. The pain of staying in a job that feels misaligned with my values is too much to bear.

~ ~ ~

The search for purpose in life is likely a question we've all pondered. Some schools of thought suggest that our life's purpose isn't necessarily tied to what we do but rather how we do it. How we move through life and radiate our unique gifts, embodying our individual frequencies, may be more important than the specific actions we take or the "jobs" we have.

If you're looking for a higher purpose, consider this: reflect on the darkest time in your life and contemplate how you can help others navigate similar challenges. That's precisely what led me to write this book.

I have discovered several spiritual tools that have helped me gain a deeper understanding of my unique frequency, the gifts I am here to share with the world, and the way I am meant to share them. If interested in diving deeper, refer to *Support Tool 5: Clues to Discovering Our Purpose.*

Craving Scenario: I Want a Fun Drink

Sometimes it's as simple as wanting something fancy, tasty, and pretty to sip on that can make us crave alcohol. Alcohol is often portrayed as fun and glamorous, with fancy garnishes to make it a treat for the senses. I used to love visiting "cool" cocktail bars and exploring all the creative flavor combinations. I loved a Corpse Reviver No. 2 and felt fancy when I figured out how to make a good one at home. I also got "picky" with my wines in front of people, pretending that I preferred my Sauvignon Blanc to be from the Marlborough region of New Zealand. But let's be real— when I was alone, I'd drink whatever cheap white wine was within arm's reach. For a while, I got into hard kombucha, convincing myself it was somehow a "healthier" choice, and I had a phase with fancy dry ciders, which made my drinking habit feel a little more upscale. Honestly, I'm laughing and rolling my eyes at myself as I write this— it's wild what we justify when drinking is our priority.

Even taking a trip to the bodega to choose what I'd drink that night used to feel like a ritual. Now, I still make that trip, but I replace it with something fun that's non-alcoholic. It's become a treat for me. Honestly, I don't even look at prices anymore because waking up without a hangover is fucking priceless.

My taste buds experienced extreme boredom when I first stopped drinking. There was that empty void of having something to do. I missed seeking out fun drinks and mixing them at home. The ritual of going to the store and crafting an interesting drink had to continue. I was used to physically having a fun drink in my hand in the evening. I started to get creative, making flavored drinking vinegars, herbal teas, extracts, bitters, sparkling teas, and homemade kombucha and kefir.

Taking the focus off alcohol made me shift my focus to what other natural ingredients I could drink that would benefit and heal my body instead of annihilating it with poison. I started designing beverages intuitively, based on what my body felt it needed at the time, both physically and energetically. Since I was not drinking, I became incredibly in tune with my emotions in response to my own needs. In fact, almost everything I put in my body became intentional medicine. I researched the power of herbs and kept a few key items on hand.

So, when you think about it this way, of course the transition to not drinking is going to be easier when at least your taste buds are stimulated and distracted. Go buy that $7 kombucha to put the probiotics back in your gut that you killed with alcohol. You're doing great.

To learn more about what I keep stocked now, refer to *Support Tool 6: Herbal Inspiration.*

Craving Scenario: It's All Too Much; I Wish I Weren't So Sensitive

I'm feeling incredibly sensitive today, and it's uncomfortable—like I'm on the verge of either crying or retreating into hermit mode. A drink would numb it out! But no, I've promised myself not to go down that road anymore. So, why do I feel this way? I've carried this deep sensitivity my entire life, always viewing it as a weakness. I used alcohol to fit in and mask what I was truly feeling. But what if I tried to understand it better instead of hiding from it?

I grew up believing my sensitivity was a flaw, something undesirable that I needed to hide from the world. In response, I created a "tough girl" persona during my adolescence to mask that part of myself. I'm already tall, which helped, and I leaned into it by adding a touch of goth and a smattering of tattoos, hoping people would see me as tough instead of sensitive. But deep down, I've always been a soft-shell crab. Using alcohol to suppress my sensitivity didn't make it disappear; it only created a deeper divide within me, delaying the process of reconnecting with my authentic self.

I found a documentary on the Gaia network called *Sensitive*. It stated that 15-20% of people are considered Highly Sensitive People, or HSP. There's a coined *name* for this?! I felt seen, heard, and not so alone. I also read an incredible book called *I Don't Want to Be an Empath Anymore* by Ora North. Simply identifying myself as an empath was profoundly healing. I finally understood why simply being present to another's pain, suffering, or negativity left me feeling overwhelmed and emotionally drained, because I simply didn't know how to process it besides deeply relating to the point where I feel it as if it's my own.

Sometimes, this deep sensitivity can feel overwhelming, which can easily lead to escapism or addiction, just as it did for me. When you're highly sensitive, you often absorb other people's negative energy like a sponge, making it difficult to distinguish between what's yours and what belongs to someone else. This constant emotional influx can feel exhausting, leaving you searching for ways to cope or numb the intensity of it all. I no longer had to numb myself when I gained a deeper understanding of this gift and how to work with it, not against it.

As with so much in life, it's possible to shift your perspective from negative to positive. Instead of viewing my sensitivity as a weakness, I reframed it as a superpower. Being an HSP or empath is a doorway to profound emotional, energetic, and environmental sensitivity. This gift allows us to translate subtle cues from the world into intuitive insights. It lets us experience life on a deeper level and empowers us to make meaningful contributions to the world through reflection. Our sensitivity provides valuable insight about what to embrace or avoid, helping us set boundaries and create environments that support our well-being. Emotional depth can fuel creativity, deep compassion, and make us exceptional friends, leaders, and lovers. Sensitivity isn't a burden— it's a gift.

Through deeper exploration on the topic of sensitivity, I learned techniques for protecting my energetic space by grounding, clearing, and protecting. This has become a daily ritual I never skip. Every morning in the shower, I take time to ground myself, clear away any unwanted energies, and set up a protective energetic boundary for the day ahead. I also try to repeat this practice every evening and add an extra layer of protection whenever I find myself in overwhelming or crowded situations, such as on the subway. It's worth noting that the more personalized you make this practice, the more effective it will be for you. Trust your intuition and go with what feels right for your energy.

For more details on energetic hygiene practices, refer to *Support Tool 3*. If you relate to this chapter on Sensitivity, I would encourage you to look into a few aspects of your Astrology chart, as well as the centers in Human Design, described in *Support Tool 6: Human Design*.

Using Astrology to Understand Emotional Sensitivity

I am not an astrologer but I was able to understand these concepts through my own research. This is just one small aspect of what astrology can reveal for you. I encourage you to get a full astrology reading by a trained professional for a deeper dive.

In astrology, your birth chart is divided into 12 houses— like slices of a pie— each representing a different area of life. Emotions and sensitivity are most closely associated with the water houses: the 4th, 8th, and 12th. These houses correspond to the water signs Cancer, Scorpio, and Pisces, and are linked to themes like home and family (4th), emotional transformation and intimacy (8th), and the subconscious and spiritual connection (12th).

Sensitivity shows up uniquely for each person, shaped by the entire chart and the aspects between planets. Key influences on emotional expression include the Moon sign (emotions and instincts), Rising sign (how you move through the world), Venus (how you give and receive love), and Neptune (spiritual and emotional sensitivity). Exploring the signs and placements of these elements can reveal important layers of your emotional nature. Water signs— Cancer, Scorpio, and Pisces— are especially known for their emotional depth and intuitive perception.

When I discovered that half my chart is water signs and very prevalent in the houses I just discussed, I finally understood that my sensitivity wasn't a flaw— it was part of my nature. I stopped resisting it and trying to be someone I wasn't.

Craving Scenario: Why Did I Agree to This Again? I'm Burnt Out.

I really don't want to go to this social thing tonight, I have zero interest in this side gig tomorrow, and that big favor I reluctantly agreed to? Regretting it already. Cue the alcohol craving— because in the past, I drank to make myself forget for a moment I said yes to all the things I didn't actually want to do. Why is saying no so damn hard? Why do I feel the need to be constantly busy?

I used to drink to muffle the drained feeling of overcommitment— to give myself fake energy to push through things I didn't actually want to do, to sustain the people-pleasing that was draining me. I drank to convince myself I wanted to do something when, deep down, I didn't want to do it at all. I've realized that it takes two or three times the energy to complete things when I force myself into something that doesn't align with me. On the flip side, if I'm doing something that lights me up, it's the opposite— I can go for hours, completely energized, without hesitation or burnout.

Why is it so hard to say *no*? I've asked myself this more times than I can count. I've said yes when my whole body was screaming *no*, and I've done it for all kinds of reasons I didn't always want to admit. Sometimes it's just easier to avoid any potential tension— saying yes smooths things over, keeps the peace. No arguments, no awkward silences. Other times, it's the FOMO (Fear Of Missing Out)— like if I say no, I'll miss some magical moment or connection. That feeling can twist your arm, make you agree to things even when you're exhausted or just not into it. Then there's the part of me that wants to be liked. I want people to think I'm kind, helpful, and dependable. So I smile and nod, even when I'm quietly betraying myself. It's like I forget I have permission to choose what's right for me. Boundaries? Still learning those. Still figuring out where I end and someone else begins, and how to stand firm without feeling like a bad person. I'm still learning that saying no isn't rejection, it's self-respect. It's not cruelty, it's clarity. But damn, some days it's still so hard.

We must learn to say no, as if our life depends on it. Because it does.

Deep, sober reflection on this topic was needed for me to uncover and heal deeper issues. WHY am I a people pleaser with no boundaries? The sobering truth was the realization that I had incredibly low self-worth, and I would agree to pretty much any job or anything that people asked of me because that meant that they "needed" me. An even more profound reflection of why I've always felt this way was related to specific childhood trauma relating to rejection from a sibling. Coming to this realization was a significant step in reclaiming my confidence, and I found therapy to be helpful in the process.

An extension of the word "no" is a boundary. When I got mostly sober, I realized I had little to no boundaries set in my life. I can think of countless times I overcommitted— saying yes to more activities or social interaction than I had the energy for, getting stuck working long hours, and in a shitty mood on top of it all because I wasn't honest with myself. I was also guilty of overcommitting to myself, piling on unrealistic expectations of what I could accomplish in a day or week. Now, I give myself plenty of time and space to complete tasks.

Why do we feel the need to stay busy? Let's break it down to unlearn it.

- **Productivity = Worth:** This is a toxic myth, and it's absolutely not true. Your worth isn't measured by how busy you are or how much you accomplish.

- **Cultural Conditioning of Capitalism and Hustle Culture:** From a young age through school, we're conditioned by society to work a certain number of hours and constantly be busy. This is all designed to fuel capitalism and make the rich richer. We don't need to buy into this. Fuck that.

- **Fear of Falling Behind:** Stop comparing yourself to others. You're exactly where you're supposed to be on your journey— your path is uniquely yours, and there's no rush. Relax.

- **Discomfort with Stillness:** What are you running from? Stillness can be uncomfortable because it forces us to confront what we've been avoiding. But there's power in being present and sitting with ourselves.

- **External Validation:** It's easy to get caught up in seeking external validation, but real fulfillment comes from within. Be your own cheerleader, lover, mother, or father.

Our lives have a limit to what they can hold energetically. Most of us live very full lives, with every minute of our schedules spoken for. It's okay to have empty space in our schedules—really. Let's stop the glorification of being busy.

If you're reading this chapter, I challenge you to *go cancel a plan*. Say **NO** to that thing you agreed to, that you never wanted to do in the first place. Then fill that time with something you really want to do instead. That thing that genuinely lights you up. And while you're doing that thing you really wanna do instead, think about how you would feel if you were doing the thing you cancelled.

~ ~ ~

I've noticed that my energy, my true life-force energy, comes from deep within my soul. The deeper my alignment with my activity, and the more it excites me, the more effortless it becomes to complete.

I like to think of my energy reserves as an energetic cup, and my goal is to keep it as full as possible. A simple way to check in with your energy is through visualization. Close your eyes, take a few deep breaths, and imagine your body as a large cup. Observe the water inside— what color is it? How full is it? Notice how the water level shifts throughout the day.

It's important to be aware of what fills your cup and what depletes it. Of course, simply living life is going to take some energy out of that cup every day, whether it's your daily commute, chores, or necessary daily interactions. Some activities drain more than others, like a stressful conversation or intense mental focus. Even the way we show up in the world matters— forcing ourselves to fit in takes far more energy than living authentically. Holding onto resentment or unresolved emotions can also be a constant, unseen drain on one's energy.

Filling your energetic cup is essential for balance, avoiding burnout, and nurturing your soul. Simple, intentional actions can replenish your energy, such as spending time in nature, being with animals, enjoying solitude or the company of loved ones, reading, creating, cooking, or simply pausing to breathe deeply. Small moments, like a walk on your lunch break, listening to music, laughing, or sipping a warm cup of tea, can make a big difference. The key is identifying what truly nourishes you— and making it a daily priority.

We've all heard the term "soul-sucking" when describing something deeply out of alignment with our values. This isn't just a figure of speech— it's a signal. Paying attention to where our energy goes is crucial because our cup should be overflowing before we give our energy to others.

If I let my energetic cup run dry and continue to push forward, burnout is inevitable. When I'm drained, I become irritable, disconnected, and honestly, not great to be around. And who does that serve? Absolutely no one. Taking care of our energy reserves isn't selfish— it's necessary. Only when our cups are full can we show up in the world as our best, most present selves.

It's important to remember that our energy radiates outward, influencing the environment around us. Whether consciously or unconsciously, people in the room can feel your energy, mood, and emotions. Your energy sends ripples throughout the universe, affecting not only your experience but also those of others.

If you're running on empty— whether it's from depleted energy reserves or a drained emotional cup— this can create negative energy that affects you and everyone you interact with. Operating from a place of emptiness doesn't serve you or the people around you. That's why taking care of yourself first is essential. You cannot pour from an empty cup. Prioritize your well-being, recharge, and nurture your energy so that you can show up fully for yourself and others.

I realized this power while working on a long and exhausting film project you might have heard of, called *Stranger Things*. This job required me to work 12-hour days for eight months straight. My cup was running nearly empty every day, or for a simpler way to put it, I was burnt the fuck out. A regular night's sleep, or even a "regular" weekend, no longer replenished me. My nights consisted of drinking heavily to "relieve" the stress of the day, absolutely not refilling my cup in a healthy way. One day, when I was in a dark, depressed mood (which I thought I was hiding), my highly intuitive work partner pointed out that she could feel my awful mood and it was making her uncomfortable. She said something like, "You are powerful; you don't realize how powerful your energy is." In that moment, I understood that although she could verbalize how my energy affected the room, most people could not. But just because most people cannot or choose not to verbalize something like that does not mean they can't be affected on an energetic or subconscious level.

I think I spent two months in bed recovering from that job. I contemplated for years— is that all-or-nothing lifestyle really worth it? I earned great paychecks during that time, but I completely lost connection with who I was and what I needed to be whole. Or looking back, did I ever even *learn* it??

So, how do we decide what's worth our energy or not? For a deeper dive, refer to the chapters *Creating the Life You Want Without Alcohol,* and *Support Tool 4: Tricks to Navigate a New Life.*

Craving Scenario: I Just Want to Fucking Party

I'm in a great mood, and I want to take it even higher and have fun— I just want to fucking party. Drinking will take this up a notch! But no. Pause. Sit with it. This is just an old habit talking... time to break the cycle. Why does my brain work like this?!

This builds on the *Craving Scenario: I'm Fucking Bored* by recognizing that we can invite peace into our lives, not boredom. We can let fun back into our lives in a way that's real, grounded, and doesn't need to be soaked in booze or highs to feel good. But let's be honest— when you're in that in-between space, where your old coping habits aren't running the show but the new ones haven't fully settled in yet, it can be confusing as hell. You are recalibrating your fun levels, so be patient.

Imagine fun existing on three levels:

- **Level 1 Fun** is calm and enjoyable—think reading a book, having a cozy night in, doing something creative, listening to music, meditating, or taking a leisurely walk.

- **Level 2 Fun** is more engaging, like social gatherings/laughing with friends, dancing, intentional physical intimacy, or a healthy spontaneous adventure.

- **Level 3 Fun** is the high-intensity, adrenaline-fueled kind—those extreme highs where you feel almost euphoric, whether from an exhilarating experience or substances that artificially spike your dopamine. Alcohol, drugs, porn, gambling, social media, sugar, junk food, excessive shopping.

If we've conditioned ourselves to chase Level 3 fun constantly, we may struggle to recognize or appreciate Level 1 fun when it's in front of us. It takes time to rewire our expectations and embrace a more balanced way of enjoying life. The key is counter-balancing the quick hits of Level 3 'fun' with longer and more fulfilling enjoyment from Level 1 and 2 experiences.

It's important to remember that short-term dopamine bursts lead to dopamine crashes, which can make you feel drained, anxious, or empty afterward. Every high comes with an equal and opposite low— it's the natural balance of the universe, yin and yang in action. Personally, I'd rather live in the steady, sustainable joy of Level 1-2 fun than chase the highs of substance-induced Level 3 and deal with the lows that follow.

You can have fun without being truly happy, and you can be happy without constantly seeking fun.

Let's try to notice and appreciate more of the Level 1 Fun in our lives. Many people chase "fun" as a way to manufacture happiness, but if the happiness isn't already there, the fun won't fill the gap. That's why some of the most "fun" times— wild nights out, reckless adventures, over-the-top experiences— can still leave people feeling empty (and often far worse) afterward.

Conversely, true happiness doesn't require constant fun. Someone who is deeply happy can enjoy sustained stillness, solitude, or simple pleasures without always seeking elevated levels of excitement. They don't need external highs to validate their joy.

Ultimately, the key is balance. Fun can enhance happiness, but it can't replace it. Are you seeking fun to *add* to your happiness, or to mask the lack of it?

~ ~ ~

There's a kind of happiness that's all about the quick hit— the rush. **Hedonic happiness**. It's chasing pleasure and dodging pain like your life depends on it. And yeah, it feels amazing... for a minute. The TV show marathons, the retail therapy, the hookups, the wild nights out, the highs— chemical or otherwise. It's escape wrapped in sparkle. Sometimes it's fun. Sometimes it's numbing. But it always fades. And afterward, there's often this hollow echo, like, *Was that it?*

Then there's the other kind. The slower burn. **Eudaimonic happiness**. This one asks more of you— it asks for your soul. It's not about feeling good all the time, but about living in a way that *means* something. It's making things, committing to a bigger vision, stumbling through the hard parts, showing up for people you care about, and most of all, showing up for yourself. It's not as flashy, but it's solid. Quietly radiant. The kind of joy that doesn't vanish when the party's over.

And maybe the hardest part? Learning to stop chasing the high and start trusting the depth.

~ ~ ~

Another reason we may crave an altered state of consciousness is our desire for a spiritual connection to Source energy. Once we allow ourselves to experience the natural highs and lows of life, we can experience life as altered consciousness, riding the waves of what it has to offer. To revisit this concept, refer back to *The Spiritual Effects of Alcohol* in *Part 1*.

Craving Scenario: I Want to Connect with People, but How?

This loneliness is starting to hit hard, but everyone I know drinks. At this point in my journey, it would be difficult to hang out with friends and not drink, which only makes me feel more disconnected, which makes me want a drink even more! This loop is a recipe for some melancholic crazy-making! Maybe I can call a friend, that seems safe.

Navigating social life while newly sober was incredibly difficult for me. If I reached out to an old friend to hang out, chances were, they'd be drinking, and I'd be trying to stay sober. At first, my willpower wasn't strong enough, so I had to avoid seeing friends altogether to stay on track. Instead, I connected with others in sober-conscious groups or called friends on the phone, keeping a safe distance from situations where alcohol was involved.

In every sober-conscious online group I'm part of, there's a recurring longing for the social aspect of drinking that many feel they've lost in sobriety. I've read so many stories about people losing friendships and even marriages after deciding to get sober, especially when the other person didn't make the same choice. I've experienced it too, but we must remind ourselves— no matter how tough it feels in the moment— that we are LEVELING UP our lives and our social circles for the better. It takes time to adjust to this new way of life. Try to stay positive and patient!

Sober social life is not going to be the same, so let's release that expectation immediately. It's going to look different and take more effort at first. We were so used to the easy, fake social lubrication alcohol provided, but let's not forget how fake that was. I can't count the number of drunk nights I thought I'd made a seemingly unbreakable bond with someone and thought we would be best friends, only never to see them again. I've got so many numbers saved in my phone that I honestly have no idea who the person is.

I loved the music and dancing that went along with the nightlife scene, but I had to take a break from it to limit the cravings (more on this in the *Even Music is Triggering Me?! Craving Scenario*). It was honestly heartbreaking at first. I couldn't just do the same things I always did, minus the booze, and that was an extremely hard pill for me to swallow. So, I would find my daytime friends. My coffee people. I value my coffee and breakfast people so much, because it means they're not hungover. Yoga, brunch, walks, hikes, museums, gardens— those became my new scenes. I traded my craving for nightlife for a craving for nature, and suddenly, New York began to feel out of alignment with what I was craving (cut to *Craving Scenario: I Can't Do NY Sober*). While I think there's a shift happening toward more alcohol-free nighttime options, until that becomes a little more popular, I'll take my kombucha and coffee dates, thank you.

It was important to me to find sober people because it's about so much more than whether they're drinking or not in the moment. It's about core values and how you live your lives. Every day, I consciously make an effort to be intentional about my physical and mental health and well-being, and I choose to surround myself with others who understand, recognize, and share the same values. Friendship can only go so deep if your core values are not similar. Find your tribe!

Making friends seems to get harder as we get older, and finding a community of like-minded people was a challenge for me. Many sober events seem to be closely related to spirituality. As you are now aware, I am a deeply spiritual person, but it is a highly personal journey for me. Spiritual events often feel too organized or cult-like for me. In New York, it was hard to find activities or social situations that weren't either entirely centered on alcohol or veering into spiritual territory. Where's the neutral ground of events that aren't centered around alcohol and not centered around spirituality? So, I decided to take matters into my own hands. I started a WhatsApp group called Sober.NYC. A place to share alcohol-free events and offer a sense of community where we can connect, share experiences, and receive encouragement on our journey towards a healthier relationship with alcohol. Something like this may already exist where you live, but why not start it yourself if it doesn't? Create the things you wish existed.

~ ~ ~

As time progresses, I find that I prefer my social time to be one-on-one with close friends or in very small groups. I much prefer deeper, meaningful conversations and connections, as opposed to shorter, fleeting moments or small talk that's necessary in larger group or party situations.

I've also found that I'm truly happy being alone for longer periods. My energy and vibration are sacred to me, and I am much more aware and protective of them without the alcoholic cloud. I am very picky about who I share my energy field with. If the vibes are not right for me, I have no problem removing myself from a person's energy field or an uncomfortable situation. If I'm being honest, most of the time, I would prefer a walk in nature rather than time with another human, particularly one who is not a vibrational match.

My viewpoint of what a social life "should be" was so influenced by alcohol that it took almost two years to come up with my own definition. Upon deeper reflection, I realized that I had unconsciously held the belief that extroverts are more valuable than introverts due to societal conditioning. Extroverts are often seen as more successful or desirable because they thrive in social situations, easily make connections, and tend to be more vocal. By nature, that is not me. Release of judgment and comparison, along with a deep acceptance of my introverted nature, was necessary to move past this conditioning.

Tune in to what *you* want to do. Everything else is nonsense.

When we are in this transition phase between quick drunk connections being the norm to trying to build more lasting relationships with a foundation, it can feel incredibly lonely, and I get it, deeply. But I quickly learned that those connections that lasted a night weren't fulfilling. When I started living more authentically, I found myself drawn to fewer people and embracing my newfound natural hermit mode. The more I embraced my solitude, the more I understood that real connection stems from inner peace, not from using others to fill a void.

Craving Scenario: But it Will Make Me Social!

So, I show up to a party sober and awkward as hell. I consider myself mostly an introvert, but I do appreciate my people time here and there. There are some drinks just sitting over there in that cooler. Maybe I'll just grab one and it'll make me less awkward and more social. But what if I didn't... what if I leaned into this awkward feeling instead of running away from it, for once in my fucking life?

I've been in this situation many times, and I have experienced working through and resisting this craving, and also succumbing to it. Both have been valuable learning experiences.

I finally realized that the idea that alcohol makes me social was just a story I told myself. So what if I'm a little quiet? I'll speak when it feels right, when the conversation is meaningful, not just to fill the silence with drunken nonsense. No one is analyzing my awkwardness except me. Why not lean into it? Or take a deep breath and move on. Ask a damn question. Give a damn compliment. *Of course,* being sober in social settings took practice for me, because I rarely did it in my adult life!

Honestly, I suck at small talk. I want to dive into your hopes, your dreams, your goals, or your deep, dark, dirty shit. Let's get vulnerable. Alcohol made me okay with surface-level bullshit, but why did I even care about being good at that? I realized at the end of one of these experiments, maybe the booze wasn't for socializing— maybe it was just numbing my *own boredom.* Woah.

After surviving 2-3 hours at the party on nothing but soda water, I start to notice the shift— the crowd getting louder, sloppier, dumber. Is *this* what I thought I was missing? I wanted to fit in with *this*? Is *this* what I used to look like all those years? The realization hits hard. I make a swift exit before getting too annoyed, leaving on a high note, proud of my clarity.

It was truly eye-opening when I first experienced this vibrational mismatch. Alcohol lowers your vibration, and as a sober person surrounded by drunk people, I felt completely out of sync. These weren't authentic interactions— they were distorted, exaggerated, *fake as hell*. Alcohol turns you into someone you're not, even if it's a seemingly happier version. But forced happiness is still fake, and I'm not about that fake life anymore. I'd rather be home alone in my truth than surrounded by artificially amplified personas. Thanks, but no thanks.

On the flip side, I've given in and had a drink or two at these parties. I'm human, and every choice is a learning experience. I believe we have a finite amount of willpower each day, and maybe on those nights, mine was already depleted before I even walked in. It's also wise to explore: *Why am I going to this party?* If I am seeking a genuine human connection, I try to make sure I have a sober buddy or at least go early before the crowd becomes a vibrational mismatch. Entertainment, music, dancing, and networking are also healthy reasons. But if I want to go because I am trying to escape a shitty day and get a hit of dopamine, this could be a red flag and there is an unaddressed need lurking beneath the surface. And that's when I find myself giving in to a drink when I am avoiding my problems.

On a weak day, resisting temptation feels nearly impossible, especially in a crowd unaware of my sober journey, where I feel practically invisible. Every time I've given in and had a drink when I told myself I wouldn't, the outcome is the same. I expect to be more fun and social, but instead, the drink makes me sluggish and dull. Since I'm less accustomed to alcohol now, I can actually feel my brain slowing down, my body becoming toxic, and my energy sinking. Instead of feeling more social, I feel worse than before I even had the drink. It was all in my head that alcohol would make me more engaging, because, in reality, I end up reverting to small talk and becoming exactly what I don't like!

Being able to witness both sides of this experience is truly a gift, and I encourage you to conduct your own experiments. Stay grounded, stay present, and observe— not just what's happening within you but also the energy of the group as a whole. If you choose to drink, do it consciously and pay attention to the subtle effects. If the vibe isn't right or people start to annoy you, or if you feel uncomfortable for any reason at all, give yourself permission to LEAVE. Your time on this earth is fucking precious— act like it.

Craving Scenario: I Want to Drink to Tolerate This Person

Sometimes the craving to drink doesn't come from wanting to feel good— it comes from not wanting to feel *them*. Their energy. Their presence. Their pain. Their chaos. Or maybe just the dull, empty space between you and them that used to be filled with something, anything, other than awkward silence.

I didn't always notice this. At first, it just felt like, *Oh, I need a drink to loosen up... to have fun...* because that's what we always did together. But what I was really doing was drinking to endure someone I didn't want to be around. Someone whose relationship had no real depth to begin with— a connection built more on habit, distraction, or convenience than actual emotional resonance. And that's a brutal truth to face, especially when it's someone you're in deep with— romantically, platonically, or by blood.

This scenario cracks open the uncomfortable space where people-pleasing, guilt, and self-abandonment meet substance use. And if you've ever used alcohol as social armor, you'll get it. This one's for the moments where the question becomes: *Is it the person I want to escape, or am I not ready to face the truth about this relationship?*

Romantic

I've been in a couple of romantic relationships where I found myself drinking to tolerate being around the person— an obvious sign (in hindsight) that they were the wrong relationships. But by the time I realized it, I was already in deep, living with them. Admitting this to yourself takes a lot of honesty, but if you can catch yourself doing it, that's step one toward change.

When I recognized myself doing this in my early twenties, I took a trip to Europe— part with my brother, part solo. As part of the trip, I worked on an organic avocado, almond, and olive farm. With no easy access to alcohol, my almost daily drinking habit came to a halt, and in hindsight, that was the best thing that could have happened. The sober solitude gave me the clarity to reflect— was I craving just a little more space from this person, or did I need permanent space? It turns out that I missed him very little, and I ended the relationship soon after.

The other relationship that triggered my drinking was the one right before I got mostly sober. He would repeat the same stories of his trauma over and over, and I felt like his trauma dumpster. He needed more than just a loving partner to listen— he needed real, professional help— but he wasn't ready to receive it. The weight of carrying his pain alongside my own was too much, so I drank to avoid feeling any of it. But that coping mechanism wasn't sustainable, and eventually, I had to remove myself from the situation.

Friends

We all have those friends. The ones you get fucked up with. It's what you have *always* done together, and you think you're going to do it together until the day you die! Then you get mostly sober, and your priorities change. But they don't change with you. It almost feels like you have to choose between having friends or being sober and alone. It's fucked up but a painful part of the necessary process.

I attempted to switch it up and hang out sober. Surely, with such a long-standing friendship, there had to be something more than just getting fucked up together, right? The unclouded information was shocking and simple. I do not prefer this person's company when I'm sober. What I was passive or complacent about when I was drunk, now annoys me. I'm allowed to change my preferences. I'm not forcing anything that doesn't feel right. It's truly as simple as that— end of story.

So, how about sober buddies? I met a friend through a mutual friend's parties when we were both still drinking. We ended up cutting out alcohol within a month of each other, separately! It was great! We were each other's sober buddies when we went out dancing together. That relationship, sober, lasted about a year. Then I began to see him as the real him, which was incredibly superficial, ego-driven, and controlled by money, rather than genuine happiness. Upon realizing our different inherent values, my interactions with him could only go so deep. I noticed that I had to lower my vibration to be around him. It was an interesting observation. Did I really want company this badly, to keep it surface level with someone I'd known for years? An incident occurred where I felt manipulated for his benefit, and I used that as an opportunity to break free from the friendship, as I felt like I was giving more than receiving. It felt as if the universe was clearing the way for friends in better alignment to enter.

Family

Upon getting mostly sober, I realized I was using alcohol to tolerate being around a certain family member as well. So, when I removed alcohol as a crutch for their company, I started to pay attention to *how I felt* around them, and it was quite shocking at first. Attempting to hang out one afternoon was absolutely exhausting. At one point, their energy was so incredibly draining, I felt like I had to go take a nap halfway through the amount of time we were "supposed to be" spending together. I realized we are just too different in the way that we communicate, and being sober made me see so clearly exactly how. I operate from a place of emotions, gut feelings, and intuition, while they communicate from a very logical head space. Deeply different ways of existing and communicating make even the smallest interactions seem like navigating an obstacle course. I'm not saying either of us is right or wrong, just so different.

After that experience, I realized I would never choose to be friends with this person if they weren't related to me. But alas, they are family, so they are going to be in my life to a certain extent, whether I choose it or not. I'm still pondering what level of disconnect seems to be the appropriate amount.

~ ~ ~

Every relationship is a mirror of our truth and, therefore, a fast track to healing. I have done spiritual healing work alone, but the growth is always much faster with a partner in my life. Whether they have shared spirituality with me or not, it doesn't matter. Every relationship is an opportunity to grow, learn, and heal. Relationships can reflect and amplify our trauma or can just as easily open our hearts to healing and understanding. We are not victims until we choose to view ourselves that way. Pay attention to what the relationships in your life are bringing up for you.

I have attended two group past life regression sessions (I found the offerings through my local yoga studios), as well as two at-home meditations. These regressions provided incredibly enlightening information about the relationship dynamics with two of my family members and one from a past partnership. Although you should enter past life regressions with an open mind to be receptive to what is needed at the time, what may come up for you could be valuable insight into your relationships. I thought the idea of past life regression seemed like a very far-fetched, unattainable thing until I tried it. It's simply a guided meditation. After the two in-person sessions, I felt comfortable enough to seek a guided meditation online and do it at home alone.

~~~

Relationships are sure to reflect our authenticity, and we get to choose who we prefer to be around and who we will be better off separating from.

"You are the average of the five people you spend the most time with." – Jim Rohn

Who we are around the most significantly influences who we are, shaping our personality, values, and outlook on life, essentially "adding up" to make us who we are. We truly only have space and time for a certain number of people to be actively involved in our lives, so let's choose wisely.

I want to share what it feels like when a relationship is right for me, since being mostly sober. When I'm with this person, I feel naturally high on life. We are vibrating at the same frequency, and I can feel the beautiful, equal, energetic exchange. My state of consciousness is altered, and we vibrate even higher together; a feeling of lightness and positivity is the side effect. There are so many synchronous signs that this person should be in my life, it is almost unbelievable. There is no desire to escape the presence of this person with alcohol because it is so easy to be with them. There are no games to play, and we can be completely authentic. There is deep acceptance, understanding, and safety. Getting fucked up with them would be a hindrance to the deep connectivity. *This* is what it's all about. When you find someone who can accept you and all your weirdness and who can bring out your inner child, they are your tribe. Keep them around. And be that person for them every minute that you can.

Craving Scenario: Life is Meaningless

I hate to say it, but it's true. Life is inherently meaningless unless we give it meaning. Isn't that exciting?! We get to choose our own adventure, paint our own pictures, and decide what truly matters, so let's choose wisely.

But oof, have I been there, to that dark side. Life was meaningless because that's what I had assigned to it. I thought, "If life is meaningless, then nothing I do matters. If nothing I do matters, then nobody cares (not even myself) if I drink for days on end. Might as well try to 'have fun' at the very least." The most meaning came from cheap thrills and quick highs. Friendships were made based on the desire for the same level of debauchery. Then the unsustainability backfired, plunging me deeper into that black hole called depression.

I began searching for small moments of meaning in life, shifting my belief that nothing is a mere "coincidence," but rather part of a greater synchronicity. Once I adopted this perspective, the subtle signs I encountered daily became affirmations that I am here for a purpose, on the right path, and doing what I'm meant to do.

Angel numbers, especially 11:11, 222, and 555, frequently appear in my life. When I spot them, I pause to reflect on my current thoughts or actions, knowing that for me, it's a sign that I am living in alignment.

I also had a dream where I was told, "If you're lost, follow the three pyramids," so the symbol of a pyramid has become significant for me. Notice the recurring symbols in your life and the meaning they hold for you. You can assign your own interpretations, or you might explore their traditional meanings. The way you connect with these symbols is entirely up to you.

Tiny sparks of meaning can also be cultivated through mindfulness. Taking time to appreciate the beauty in simple things, like a plant or flower, a warm cup of tea, a piece of ripe fruit, or the glow of a sunset. Even mundane tasks can become mindful moments. Feel the water flow over your hands while washing dishes, or the softness of a fluffy towel fresh from the dryer. The key is simply to notice. To be in the now.

The tiny sparks of meaning I began to notice snowballed into something much greater. As I appreciated the smaller synchronicities, I began to recognize the larger ones, each carrying its own inherent value and ultimately adding to the value and meaning of my life. Think about the people in your life, or even the random encounters you've had. The chain of events required for two people to cross paths and share an experience on this planet is truly mind-boggling. When I began to understand how unique each moment is, I found myself appreciating things so much more, and that appreciation evolved into deep gratitude.

I started to shift my focus to what I had instead of what I didn't have. A roof over my head, food in the fridge, a body that works pretty okay, the ability to take care of myself, people who have my back— stuff I used to take for granted. Gratitude wasn't some fluffy spiritual practice; it was survival. A way to keep my head above water when things felt heavy. The more I paid attention to the good, the more I realized my life wasn't empty—it was actually very full.

After starting with small hits of mindfulness and gratitude, then came the search for deeper meaning for the bigger picture of my life. The search for my true purpose and life themes became a real passion of mine on this journey, and I'd love to share what I've found. For practical ways to guide you towards discovering your purpose, refer to *Support Tool 5*.

Craving Scenario: Let's Celebrate!

Not all cravings come from negative places, and it's interesting to recognize the full spectrum. Upon hearing the news that I had landed my most recent film job, I felt genuinely happy at the time, and I wanted to celebrate with a drink. I wanted to go out and order champagne, because that's how we are taught to celebrate as a society. With poison! How sad is that?

What started as a happy, celebratory moment quickly turned into a sense of sadness about our culture. We're conditioned to put literal poison into our bodies when we celebrate. I reminded myself that this isn't the way to carry the good vibes from the news. I will no longer follow this societal norm. I will value and respect my body more than the general public even knows how to. I reminded myself that I probably wouldn't stop at just one drink. I would feel awful after having more than one, since my body wasn't used to it anymore. I reminded myself that the trash feeling would have residual emotional effects, including regret and a lowered vibration.

I shared my good news with close friends and family, posted about my craving in my Sober.NYC WhatsApp chat, grabbed some chocolate and a sparkly N/A drink, and rode the craving wave to the other side. The next morning, I was so grateful I made that choice.

Craving Scenario: I Want to Numb This Grief

Someone in my life has passed. Why her?! She was such a ray of sunshine; the world needed her. I want to fucking numb it out with alcohol. I don't want to feel this emptiness anymore. This hole in my heart from someone taken too soon. How great it would be to go to the store, get a bulk discount deal of my trash beverage of choice, and numb out all these confusing feelings. No. We've been mostly sober long enough to know that this is not the way. Numbing out your feelings will only delay the healing process. You know this. Be strong enough to let the craving pass through you. Go deeper into the feeling instead...

Grief turns into anger for the unjustness of life. The awareness of our impermanence turns back at you like the most terrifying mirror.

So many difficult emotions. But *why* are those emotions bubbling up? Because we LOVED those people. Those people brought such light and joy into the world. So, is the true underlying emotion here actually LOVE, not grief? In this moment, I am allowing the grief, sadness, and anger to wash through me, but I am choosing to lean into the underlying reason for these emotions: *love*. I wouldn't have been able to feel these other "negative' emotions if I didn't feel the love for her in the first place. Love turns into gratitude for the wonderful times we shared. This opens my heart to greater appreciation and awareness of what I have in my life. To connect with the people that are important to me, and tell them I love them, because it can be lost in an instant.

I would have never come to this sense of loving peace if I had reached for a drink when my negative feelings were taking over. I would've silenced the signal instead of listening to the message. The urge to drink was just a flash. A panic response. An escape route. But staying put, staying present, letting the feelings wash through me— that's what allowed me to access a kind of peace that isn't temporary. It's the peace that comes from meeting yourself fully, even in the mess. If I had reached for a drink, I would've delayed that moment of clarity. Maybe by a night. Maybe by months. Maybe I would've never gotten there at all. And that's what alcohol always stole from me without me realizing it— the chance to *really* feel, *really* heal, and *really* find peace that sticks.

Is it starting to make sense yet?

Craving Scenario: Even MUSIC is Triggering Me?! Can I Live?!

Electronic music has been a huge part of my life since I was 15. In the first three months of getting mostly sober, I couldn't even listen to house music— it was so incredibly triggering. It went hand in hand with partying and drinking for over 20 years of my life. I was freaking out. Was it all FAKE?! Do I not even like house music at ALL?! Who was I without it? It felt like a full-blown identity crisis.

When I stopped drinking, I got on a folk-rock kick. Anything with a synth sounded too much like a party to me, and it was immensely triggering. I wasn't sure if my entire personality was changing just because my musical tastes shifted after getting mostly sober. It was something I had to let go of— whatever changes were happening, I knew not drinking was the right choice. In the end, I just needed to change the music I listened to during those sensitive first few months to stop me from thinking about partying the way I used to. I'm honestly much more open-minded to lots of different music as a result.

Before getting mostly sober, I needed music playing in the room or earbuds when I was out, almost all the time. I always had a party in my ear while walking around the streets of New York. Deep, bassy, sexy, dirty house, always digging for new music and the next hot shit party to go to— like Claude Vonstroke, Green Velvet, Justin Martin, Shiba San, Disclosure, Steve Darko, VNSSA, Holt 88— some serious party music. It was almost as if being alone with my own thoughts was not okay. Oh... it wasn't.

It was only when I stopped drinking that I became okay with empty space and silence. What used to feel like a scary, empty void transformed into a kind of meditation and a completely new experience. It became beautiful to me to walk around New York and really listen to the soundscape. It was interesting and different to be in tune with my surroundings instead of drowning them out. Not to mention, safer!

A couple of years before I got mostly sober, when COVID hit NY, I missed going out, hard. I missed music and dancing so much. My boyfriend at the time taught me to DJ, and it is one of the only hobbies, besides sewing, that has held my attention. It became a fun and creative outlet, mixing two songs to create something new and interesting. Since house music has been a part of my soul since I was 15, and I've always loved to dance, DJing came naturally to me. I can feel the flow of the songs together, and my intuitive nature makes it easy for me to read the vibe of the room and know what to play. I played at some of the coolest spots in Bushwick and Williamsburg, and at one point had a twice-a-month gig. I loved it so much I'd play anywhere I could just to be able to share a vibe— block parties, various apartments, backyard, and rooftop parties.

But that DJ life can be toxic. I had DJ friends I wanted to support, so I was always out showing up for them. If I wanted to get gigs, I had to network, which meant going out a lot. And, of course, drinking was always part of the scene. Drugs too. Gigs didn't pay much, but at least there were free drinks! Balancing DJing with a full-time job was tough, especially when I had "regular" daytime hours. At one point, I was working on a 50-hour-a-week film job and trying to keep up with my Wednesday night gig. Needless to say, that didn't last long.

When I got mostly sober, I couldn't even listen to the music I used to play, let alone mix it! I'd always had drinks when I DJed, even at home, thinking it gave me more confidence. But now, I realize that was just a false sense of confidence. It felt like a huge loss, as something I loved so much became triggering, and I couldn't even enjoy it without a mega craving. Thankfully, it didn't stay that way for long. Something you love isn't going to disappear completely, although it may change shape. Just know that when it changes shape, it is aligning more authentically to the sober version of you!

Thankfully, after about three or four months, I was able to reintroduce electronic music into my life. I found a morning rave to go to, and I loved the concept. They served coffee and fun non-alcoholic drinks, and I was proud of myself for going alone. At three months sober, it was such a refreshing experience to find a group of people who loved house music and were sober together. The collective strength and desire to be healthy and have fun together was tangible.

Unfortunately, (at least for me), this event had a strange, forced spiritual element at the end. After the organizer spoke, she told us to sit on the floor and stare into a stranger's eyes for 3 minutes. It was so uncomfortable, but it would have been odd if I had gotten up and left. As you may know by now, I am an extremely spiritual person. But I don't want any spirituality to be forced on me, especially when I'm just trying to dance and have a good time! It was so weird. Let me dance in peace, and don't make me force a connection with a stranger, thanks. That's not how spirituality works, or even friendships. At least not mine.

Despite the strange end to that morning rave, it brought me back to what I loved. I started practicing DJing again, this time sober. While I felt a bit stiff at first, I knew I'd be able to hear the nuances of my mixes more clearly, and everything would flow smoother without any drunken mistakes. The fundamentals of DJing are like riding a bike, so I was able to jump right back in.

I tried to find daytime parties that I could play so I didn't have to deal with the drunken mess that nightlife inherently is. I started a new playlist called "Sober Set." It felt fake— I had some idea in my head about what a woke sober DJ would sound like, and it was boring the hell out of me. I was trying to infuse more positive, happy vibes into my music just because I was mostly sober, thinking that would be my new vibe. I don't know whose fucking formula I was trying to follow, but I wasn't being authentic. I was sober, not basic! I've always been drawn to slightly dark and grimy music, so why would that change because I stopped drinking?

It was after 14 months of being mostly sober that I finally felt like I could DJ confidently and authentically again. And today, it feels fucking good. I almost want to play out in a club badly enough to stay up late and fight the drunk crowd on the way to the DJ booth. Almost! The search continues to play daytime parties in the sun, where that nighttime drunken debauchery does not exist. But in the meantime, I'll play for my own dance party of one and throw a mix on SoundCloud for my friends once in a while.

Craving Scenario: I Feel Anxious— A Drink Will Help Me Relax

First DJ gig as a mostly sober person at one of my favorite clubs in Bushwick, Jupiter Disco. Goddamn I was so nervous. I wanted to drink since noon that day to take the edge off. But I was determined to do it sober. The club had a rotary mixer that would require a little more focused attention than digital setups, and I wanted to be present for it. Old me would be drinking and partying leading up to the gig and probably fucking something up. The new me was doing grounding and breathing exercises before the gig, reading the energy of the room, and being tuned in as fuck.

I'm much more confident in my abilities now and much more used to navigating life alcohol free, but I think I will always be a little nervous playing a bigger gig. Why? Because I care about what I'm doing and I'm a fucking human feeling human emotions. Just roll with it. In this case, maybe anxiety is just a little fact of life. Situations like this are nothing we have to drink or pop a Xanax about.

~~~

Sometimes I feel anxious for no apparent reason. When sitting with and examining your anxiety, ask, is it old, unprocessed emotions, fear of the unknown, or a sense of doom over an impending event? Is it self-imposed pressure you are putting on yourself? Are you overstimulated from either your environment or caffeine? Is it a deeper existential anxiety? Where is this discomfort sitting in your body? Do you need to move?

Emotions *must* move through the body; otherwise, they become trapped and can cause a myriad of problems. Numbing with alcohol only buries them deeper, and I had been doing that for years on top of years. The muck we buried will inevitably surface when we stop drinking. Please don't be ashamed to work through even the oldest emotional wounds, as they can come at you from all angles and when you're least expecting it. As someone who feels deeply, I know firsthand that, as uncomfortable as it is, emotions must be felt to be released.

So often, we are expected to sit still during our days, which feels incredibly unnatural to me. I like to move my body after small periods of intense focus or even during (think of pacing while we are having intense conversations). If I don't let energy move through my body regularly throughout my days, it can build over a few days, accumulating "anxiety" and therefore contributing to a craving. Nuances like this are impossible to notice if you're drinking all the time. We don't understand the source of the anxiety, but we know the quick fix— grab that drink.

Ever witnessed a dog go through something unpleasant? They will do a full body shake to shake off the negative energy and then continue their day like nothing happened. Animals instinctively do this, but as humans, we might "look weird" if we do the same. What's worse: looking weird for a few seconds or carrying around negative energy indefinitely?

117

Anxiety is a disconnection in yourself— two parts of you are not aligned, and it's as if they are fighting against each other. Perhaps the side that is your authentic, true desire, and the other side— what you *think* you should do, by way of whatever conditioning you are telling yourself. *What do you really need at this moment?* If you resonate with this, then exploring "Parts Work" might be helpful. I like Teal Swan's guided meditation on this topic, and many other therapists integrate this work.

Let it go:

Shake off that anxious energy— literally. Jump around, swing your arms wide, or put on music and dance like no one's watching. Go for a run, hit the gym, try yoga, or take a kickboxing class if your anxiety feels more like aggression.

Let it out vocally, too. Sigh, yell, groan, flutter your lips, or stick out your tongue and hiss. The weirder, the better— if it makes you laugh, even better! Just get that energy moving and release it. Screaming is underutilized. It can serve as a form of catharsis, offering a healthy outlet for bottled-up emotions and tension. Go ahead, scream into that pillow. By vocalizing our intense feelings, we often find a sense of relief and enhance our ability to manage emotions. It's like hitting an emotional reset button.

Crying is highly underrated. Did you know tears release the stress hormone cortisol from the body? If you're anxious because you are stressed, let the tears flow. It makes me so sad that crying can be looked at as a form of weakness, especially the way men are raised in our culture. Crying as an adult is incredibly brave because it gives us permission to be vulnerable, and in a way, it connects us with our inner child. It's a form of self-acceptance and an emotional release of something that no longer serves you. And that can be incredibly healing.

I was recently walking in my neighborhood on Knickerbocker Avenue in Bushwick, Brooklyn, and I was stuck behind a slow-moving mom and son. The kid was fixated on whatever sweet thing was in his hand, and he tripped on a broken umbrella and fell directly on his face. Mom immediately said, "Don't cry, get up, don't cry." It was a stark reminder of how frowned upon crying is, still, in our culture, even when you fall directly on your face. Now, what if we just went through the emotional equivalent of falling directly on our face? Society tells us to pull our shit together, hide our emotions, and act like nothing happened. Fuck that. Cry, stay home, throw yourself a pity party, whatever you gotta do to let it move through you. **Just don't drink.** Drinking caps the emotion and keeps it unprocessed and trapped in the body indefinitely, rather than moving through us in the natural way it's supposed to.

Breathe

Sometimes when I'm feeling anxious, I often realize I wasn't breathing properly— I'll notice how shallow my breathing is in that moment. It sounds obvious, but it's a game-changer and is overlooked more often than we probably even realize. Take deep, full breaths. Try box breathing: inhale through your nose for four counts, hold for four, exhale for four, then hold at the bottom for four—then repeat. Do it at least 3 times in a row. This technique shifts your body from a state of stress to one of relaxation, slowing your heart rate, relaxing your muscles, and stabilizing your blood pressure.

Meditate

Once you have let the energy go physically in whatever way feels best, sit still and try a quick guided meditation, even 5-10 minutes. There are plenty of online resources to help calm your mind and create space. At one point, I used the Headspace app and enjoyed its short, easy meditations and soothing voice. There are plenty of great options out there now to explore. If you're new to meditation, guided sessions are an excellent way to begin.

Craving Scenario: An Old Friend is in Town— Clearly, Drinks!

We don't always win against alcohol. But we can learn.

We knew each other in Atlanta, and we always partied hard together. Drinks, drugs, dancing, cigarettes, out until 3 am, all of it. He came to Brooklyn, we got lunch, and I thought I was safe from alcohol because we were meeting early in the day, and I didn't plan for it in case it was encountered in my orbit. He knew I wasn't drinking much/if any and asked if I would be ok with him ordering a drink. He said he wouldn't drink if it made me feel uncomfortable. I highly respected that, and I should have spoken my truth and said that I would prefer him not to because my willpower was weak at that moment. But instead, I said I didn't care, and I took it a step further, I got a glass, too. And then a second. And then ended up at a house party and had five more.

I'm not sure why I couldn't win this one. I had worked my ass off that week, and I felt that old pendulum pull of work hard/party hard. Maybe he triggered a very old, deep neural pathway in my brain. That desire to have fun like old times was just too strong. And I was fucking lonely. I barely had any friends left in Brooklyn because I had to separate myself from the parties. When I was drinking at that party, I wasn't even having fun anymore, but I couldn't even pinpoint why until the next day when I was fucking hungover and shameful. I was drinking largely to deal with the shitty, basic music that was being played at this party, and to try somehow to fit in with the conversations that I had no interest in. I should have left way earlier, but my good decision-making had long left the building. At least I managed to go home early-ish instead of going out with the group, where I probably would have had five more, done some drugs, and smoked some cigarettes just like old times with him.

I learned that I can rarely moderate. After two drinks, it's over; I'm probably giving in to more. And before two drinks, what's the point? We have a finite amount of willpower available to us each day, so the combination of a hard week, seeing an old friend, being lonely, and being around someone who was drinking was too much for me to fight.

Even though I had slipped up more than I wanted, I had come a *really* long way from where I was 6 months prior. This lifestyle change isn't instant; it takes trial and error. I was trying to give myself grace the next day, but I was so depressed and hungover. I didn't remember them being this dull and sad. I was doing so well, but I guess I needed the lesson. I needed to identify my areas of weakness to determine how to move forward. Where to set my boundaries more clearly and how to navigate situations like this.

Over many instances like this, I've learned that I found it too difficult in the first two years of sobriety to be around people who are drinking. I've had to separate myself almost completely from those situations. I don't have the willpower to sit there and watch a friend drink while my brain is remembering how "fun" that used to be. Why put myself through the torture?

When trying to find a middle ground with friends, I try to create scenarios that are less drinking-friendly for our meet-ups. Middle of the day, museum, garden, picnic, workout together, coffee, whatever. If they aren't willing to do those types of things with you, then are they really making an effort to support your sobriety? This kind of thinking may feel selfish at first, but don't feel guilty for asking what you need while you're going through changes to be healthier. Know your limits and stand your ground.

Craving Scenario: How the Hell Do I Date Without Drinking?

At first, it was incredibly difficult for me to separate dating and drinking. The two had always gone hand in hand. Meeting someone new? Have a drink to take the edge off. Even after a few dates, I still felt the urge to get drunk together, as if alcohol would help build a deeper connection. You know— that fake, booze-fueled bond where you spill your deepest, darkest secrets way too soon. That one.

It's so easy to meet someone at a bar for the first time, but in hindsight, I see how much of a cop-out those dates were. When you are drinking, this seems to work on the surface because it's low stakes; you believe it gets rid of your first date anxiety, and neither of you has to be all that interesting because you're going to do the fake drunk bond thing. There's no thought involved in the planning. Intelligent conversation only has to last the first drink or two until you're too buzzed to care about anything intelligent. As the drinks flow, judgment fades, and poor decisions follow. I miss nothing about this societal norm!

Honestly, there's something way more romantic about dating sober. So, you're a little anxious or nervous about the first date? It means you *care,* and that's fucking cute. Tell them what you're feeling and let it move through you. The best first dates I've had were the ones where we did literally anything other than meet at a bar. It shows that the person respects my healthy lifestyle enough to think outside the box. Try a coffee shop, a walk, a picnic, a museum, or a botanical garden— anything that allows for real connection, not just liquid courage.

In my experience, meeting at a bar for a first date while being mostly sober is dangerous territory. If you're early in your sober-ish journey, I'd recommend avoiding bars altogether. At around seven months mostly sober, I decided to meet a guy from a dating app. First red flag— he couldn't come up with anything to do besides go to a bar. We went to two bars that night, with one activity in between (which I suggested). By the second bar, after watching him down about three drinks, my willpower faded, and I caved— ordering a glass of Sauvignon Blanc (the cheap AF kind, not the good kind).

Now, I realize everyone's level of willpower is different. Maybe you can hang out with people who drink, and you are fine with not drinking. That is amazing, and I admire that! But not me that night, not within my first year of being mostly sober. There was a limit to my willpower. Although we saw each other a few more times, that first date ultimately showed me we weren't a match. He was deeply involved in party culture— drinking, nightlife, and drugs. While I liked his personality, I had already lived that life. That was my past, and I was ready to move forward.

Looking back, I see it as the universe testing my commitment to a mostly sober lifestyle, like "Are you *sure* this is what you want??" Recognizing these tests were pivotal to making real change. It would have been so easy to fall back into Brooklyn's party scene with him. What struck me most was realizing that, two years earlier, I would have been all in. But we were on different wavelengths, and we both felt it. Naturally, things just fizzled out.

I make it clear from the start of meeting someone new— I don't drink. It was in my dating app profile, so no questions were needed. When I was a heavy drinker, I wanted a partner in crime to get fucked up with, and I remember someone saying they didn't drink, and I ran the other way because I wasn't ready for that. I hoped heavy drinkers would do the same. I love it when they don't read my profile and the first message is, "Want to grab a drink?" Insert eye roll and an instant delete.

Drunk Sex vs. Sober Sex

I hate to admit it, but most of the sex I've had was under the influence of alcohol. Looking back, I can say, without a doubt, sober sex is better. Alcohol desensitized me, and I didn't even realize what I was missing. Now, I can fully experience the nuances of touch, feel energy flow and exchange, and connect on a whole different level.

I used to think alcohol made me more confident in bed, but I've realized I'm way more satisfied without it. I feel better in my body because I've done the work to truly accept and love it, not just mask insecurities with booze. I make better choices about who I share intimacy with because I'm making sober decisions based on true connections, not fake drunk bonds. My energy is wayyy more sacred to me now, and sharing it is a much bigger deal. And I'm more in tune with my boundaries— what feels right and what doesn't— because sobriety brings authenticity and the confidence to speak up.

Craving Scenario: I'm Feeling so Lost and Misunderstood

I've always felt like a "weirdo," with a deep inner knowing that I don't quite belong on this planet. Mainstream society doesn't make sense to me— I don't follow trends, I couldn't care less about celebrity drama, and I purposely avoid the news. I struggle to relate to most people, because I can't do surface level bullshit for longer than about 2.5 seconds. Oh, but you know what most humans do? Drink! That should help me fit in, right?! Wait, is it really helping me "fit in," or is it just hiding the fact that I don't like it here?

A large part of the reason why I drank was to feel like I "fit in." My heart hurts when I think about how long I chose to be inauthentic. To cover up who I was, just to be accepted by whoever was in front of me. Talk about stuff I didn't care about. To be social when I didn't feel like it. To pretend like I wasn't overwhelmed when I was. I stopped pretending and took off the mask when I got mostly sober. I couldn't put on the act anymore, and any amount of doing so was painful.

When I learned about the term "starseed," it deeply resonated with me. If there was a hint as to *why* I didn't connect with most things happening on Earth, I was going to lean into it. A starseed is a spiritual concept that refers to a soul believed to have originated from another planet, star system, galaxy, or dimension— essentially, somewhere beyond Earth. Starseeds are said to incarnate here with a specific purpose: to help raise the planet's consciousness, bring healing, and assist in humanity's spiritual evolution. Many people who resonate with being a starseed often feel like outsiders, deeply sensitive, drawn to esoteric knowledge, and driven by a sense of mission they can't always explain. Starseeds tend to exhibit certain traits or experiences that align with their cosmic origins. Here are some common characteristics:

1. Feeling different, "out of place," or alien to societal norms.

2. Difficulty connecting with traditional structures, values, or systems.

3. Strong intuition and empathy, with a natural ability to sense what others are thinking or feeling.

4. Heightened sensitivity to energy, difficulty with loud places, harsh lights, or crowded spaces.

5. Impatience, because of the slower manifestation times on Earth

6. A deep curiosity about the cosmos

7. A sense of having a higher purpose or a calling to help humanity

8. Need for solitude to recharge and process energy

9. Compassion for all life, or a sense of oneness

Although I relate to every one of these traits, I don't like to refer to myself as a "starseed." It implies that I am somehow different or special when, upon deeper meditation into this concept, every single one of us has cosmic origins. We are all interconnected with the universe. From a scientific perspective, humans and all life on Earth are made from the same elements forged in stars (such as carbon, nitrogen, and oxygen). In that sense, we are all stardust, deeply connected to the cosmos. If I believed there was any separation between humans, it would discredit this entire concept, in my opinion.

We are all capable of possessing the qualities of a starseed. If you are reading this book, you may already relate to many of them. If you are here with me, you likely want to deepen your spiritual practice and gain a deeper understanding of your origins. We are all starseeds in this human experience together.

Although I've had many of these qualities from a very young age, since getting mostly sober, some of these qualities *skyrocketed*, such as sensitivity to energy, and some appeared that were not there, such as a strong desire for a higher purpose to help humanity. This list isn't stagnant and can change for you over time. We all can develop heightened, almost superhuman sensitivities if we desire to tune into them. Or, we can choose to stay tuned in to the 3-dimensional dense material energies of the earthly experience alone. However one decides to move throughout life is right for them. Sometimes I get pulled too far into the spiritual realm, and I need to remind myself to keep one foot on Earth and take some time to enjoy being human.

Through many spiritual schools of thought (such as Dolores Cannon) and my meditations, I have learned that we often come to Earth as part of a star or soul family to assist, support, and learn from one another. The concept here is that we incarnate over and over again with the same group of souls at similar times. Some of these souls may be family in one life or partners, friends, or teachers in another.

You know someone is part of your soul family when you instantly connect with them. Perhaps you experience many synchronicities when you are with them. You are cut from a similar cosmic cloth and feel strangely familiar and comfortable with them. Time may feel warped, passing both quickly and stretching slowly. It may feel like you're looking in a mirror, because you share a very similar vibration. Being around these people can feel like "home," and their influence might be felt energetically even when not physically present.

When I feel lost or misunderstood, I connect with my soul family. Connecting with people who operate on a similar vibrational level to me, even if they are no longer present on the earthly plane, reminds me that I am not alone.

Who in your life is part of your star family?

Craving Scenario: I Can't Do New York Sober

Any city where we have drank our weight in booze in one night, mistaken random places as toilets, and had an emotional moment with a lamppost can easily echo some triggers when you walk it sober. It makes sense, as most of my fun, memorable experiences in New York have been when alcohol was involved. New York was incredibly triggering at the beginning of sobriety for this reason. I didn't even know what to do anymore that didn't involve alcohol.

In the beginning, I stayed inside a lot. Hiding from the temptation of the plethora of bars, clubs, bodegas, and liquor stores that were steps from my apartment. Although I did pretty well with this approach, I can see how a change of scenery, a city change, or even a rehab facility could be extremely beneficial at the beginning of sobriety. Separation from your daily habits, usual people, and places could be very helpful.

I've lived in a lot of different places. I'm not sure if the perfect place exists. I'm mostly sure it doesn't. There's always going to be positives and negatives about anywhere you live. You choose to live somewhere for the best collection of reasons for you, and that's the best any of us can do. For anything positive in life, there is an equal and opposite negative. The balance between yin and yang is always there; sometimes, you must look deeper to see both.

At any given time, you can choose to see the negativity or the beauty of your city. In the first couple of months of getting mostly sober, it was all too easy to see the negative. Some of the things I loved about the city seemed to go hand in hand with drinking, especially the parties and social aspects. But also, the things I didn't like about my city, I would drink to cover up! Especially in the winter. Why did the bitter cold of NY seem like a perfectly legitimate excuse to drink straight whiskey in the daytime?

On one side of the coin, New York is dirty, exhausting, mostly ugly, fuckin cold, fuckin hot, and far removed from natural nature (which has been my biggest struggle with living here). I'm not a fan of that constructed nature like Central Park— still can't escape traffic noise.

On the flip side, when you get those beautiful moments in New York, it's fucking magic. You're at the right place at the right time with the right people at an exclusive rooftop party looking out at the twinkle of the city, and you feel like you're on top of the world. You make that career connection that is serendipity, magical, and life-changing. Those blossoming spring trees on that once-dead street make you remember you're alive. That moment you can get out those fall layers that level up your outfit game and make you feel like the sidewalk is a catwalk. You find an incredible and cheap hole-in-the-wall food spot that makes you feel like you won the lottery. You attend an art show where you're surrounded by so many creatives that it's hard not to be influenced yourself. You are constantly surrounded by people who are unapologetically themselves, which inspires you to do the same. New York has a curious way of bringing out your authenticity. Weirdest outfit in the neighborhood? Fit right in! Crying on the subway? No problem, get it out, I'll hand you a tissue!

Living in New York as a heavy drinker was fucking great. With no responsibility for a car or driving anywhere at all whatsoever, I could have my after-work drink earlier, literally on the train ride home from work sometimes. So nice! With such a high concentration of bars, finding a solid happy hour was not hard. Score! As someone who loves trying new things and experimenting with flavor, I would seek out fancy, world-class cocktail bars with my drinking-enabling boyfriend at the time and make it a destination. Although I truly liked finding new flavors, liquors, and interesting drinks, let's be real, I loved getting drunk more, and that was a way to convince myself I was somehow being sophisticated about drinking.

In contrast, living in New York as a mostly sober person was a huge challenge for me, but I learned ways to adapt. I had chosen to follow through with some New York-based goals and obligations, and I figured I might as well make the most of the process. Upon getting mostly sober, my already sensitive nature was heightened 10-fold. I needed to slow down significantly and pay attention to what I needed in the moment, every moment. This concept is inherently opposite to how the fast-paced city of New York operates. Instead of trying to cram a bunch of goals or activities in one day, I gave myself much time to do them, like twice as much as I would have before. Instead of tromping around the city at top speed, I walked at a slow pace and watched all the stressed-out lemmings fly past me. It was nice to take intentional steps and notice my surroundings. I cooked slow food, waited for farmer's market purchases, and never ate on the go. I showed gratitude and respect for my food.

During my heavy drinking days, I used to spend every ounce of my energy on either making money or spending it partying, and now I find great joy in doing art that truly has no purpose except to make me happy in the moment. The anxious collective energy of NY was triggering to me, and I found little ways to counteract it and live peacefully within it, requiring focused intention and willpower.

~ ~ ~

I gained an interesting perspective when I took a trip and came back to NYC. I went to San Diego to spend some time with friends and family, but my main purpose was to assess the city and see if it was a place I could imagine myself living in.

When I got there, I could feel the New Yorker still in me: walking fast to hurry up for nothing, not paying attention to the "don't walk" signs, etc. But after a few days and some time on the beach, I got it. I blended in with the city's vibe, which was very chill and much slower than New York City's pace. I loved it.

After returning from my trip, I took a day at home for reflection and self-care, only to find myself craving a drink. I couldn't believe it. I was relaxed, revitalized, and had no obvious trigger. At first, I thought it was just being back in my apartment, but that didn't make sense— I've been almost entirely sober here. Then it hit me: it wasn't my space, it was the collective energy of NYC. The stress, the busyness, the drinking culture, the party culture— I could feel it all pressing in, disrupting my inner peace. It was inescapable. For a moment, I even considered giving in and drinking like my old ways until I moved out of New York in a few months— that's how strong it was.

Witnessing the massive contrast between the collective consciousness of the two cities became one of my greatest teachers. It's something I never would have noticed if I had been drinking my way through the trip. Sobriety has made me more attuned to my surroundings, and I am deeply grateful for that, even if it chased me out of a place that is no longer in alignment.

~ ~ ~

I knew almost instantly, upon getting mostly sober, that New York was no longer the correct fit for me. I nearly moved twice, but the ideas fizzled out for different reasons. I ultimately decided to stay until the end of my two-year lease and took a six-month film job that seemed to align perfectly with that timeline— almost like the universe was signaling that it was the right decision. I knew the last six months there would be incredibly difficult for me, but the freedom I would experience after was the motivating factor.

Even though I had a clear sense of what I needed to remove from my life, I was still uncertain about what I truly wanted to add. I was in a state of transition, shedding the old layers and habits, but not yet ready to fully embrace any singular new direction. It was like standing on the edge of a vast unknown, knowing I had to let go of the past but unsure of the future path. But I trusted that in time, the right pieces would fall into place, and the things I needed would show up when I was ready to receive them. That uncertainty, though uncomfortable, was the fertile ground for new possibilities to sprout.

Craving Scenario: I Want to Be Hungover

This might sound completely wild, but I actually miss being hungover sometimes. Stay with me.

As I write this, it's a Saturday morning after grinding through a soul-sucking 50-hour workweek in the film industry (but actively working on an exit strategy). Two years ago, I'd probably be nursing a brutal hangover. And as miserable as those mornings were, they gave me something I secretly craved— permission. Permission for rest— a basic human need. Permission to sleep in, stay inside, shut out the world with blackout curtains, order takeout, be lazy, binge-watch TV, and embrace my introverted side without guilt. Whether it was psychological or physical, that recovery time was valid.

Our culture glorifies "busyness" so much that I unknowingly used hangovers as my ticket to slow down. When I stopped drinking, I realized I didn't miss *feeling like garbage*— I missed giving myself full *permission to rest*. And I had to learn how to do that without needing a self-inflicted, abusive excuse.

Now, I honor those needs in much healthier ways. I let myself recharge by lying in the sun at a park, choosing foods that might be a treat, reading a book, writing, meditating into nothingness, or literally just staring at the wall. And okay, sometimes, I still indulge in some trash TV. But the difference is, now I don't need to poison myself first to justify taking a break, and I invite you to do the same.

The term "self-care" can sometimes seem like a selfish word, or like it's a luxury. Something we don't get to have all the time, and maybe that's true for some. Does providing yourself with self-care make you feel guilty? If so, try to rephrase it by referring to this concept as taking care of **your basic human needs**.

Craving Scenario: Escapism

I've saved this one for last because it's the most subtle and, in some ways, the hardest to admit. It can easily disguise itself as any of the other craving scenarios, making it easier to overlook. But take a moment and really reflect— are there recurring craving patterns showing up for you?

For me, my *Work Sucks Craving Scenario* was a deeper desire to escape the life I had created— something I thought I wanted, but in reality was something I had outgrown.

Why Did I Agree to this Again? I'm Burnt Out Craving Scenario was to escape doing the work to feel safe saying "no," and confronting people to set healthy boundaries.

Similarly, my *I Can't Do New York Sober Craving Scenario* was really about wanting to escape the city itself.

And *I'm Fucking Bored*— was to keep hidden the unprocessed trauma that might arise from the empty space.

Essentially, the need to escape from feelings is a large part of why many of us drink. Our souls agreed to this human experience here on earth, and let's be honest, everything can feel incredibly dense at times. The quick fix we turn to—alcohol— seems like an easy way out. But when we face those emotions and allow ourselves to feel them, we gain the power to transmute them. To be able to see the positive effects of "negative" emotions is a true superpower. When we can recognize that the tough moments sparked something positive, that is where our true power lies. Harness it and use it.

Part 4: Creating the Life You Want Without Alcohol

Society often conditions us on how we should live, how we should act, and what choices we should make. You no longer need to follow the path set by social constructs or worry about what others think you should be doing. You've outgrown it, and for that reason, quitting drinking is one of the bravest things you can do. The world has enough of the same old mindless shit. We don't need more people who numb out and shut down because they fear being seen. This is your permission slip to be unapologetically 'weird.'

Fuck social constructs and "norms." They were created to perpetuate a system that benefits the few and keeps the many distracted, serving the interests of capitalism and the wealthy elite.

Fuck what your family thinks you should do. Their opinions often come from a place of judgment and projection. They're simply passing on what they wished they had achieved or what they think you "should" have— often out of worry or fear, not love.

Fuck what your partner thinks you should do. I said it. This one can be messy, but if your partner doesn't fully support your decisions to prioritize what's best for you— your growth, your happiness— then maybe that partnership isn't serving either of you in the way it should.

And fuck what your co-workers think. Truly does not matter! Most of the time, their opinions are rooted in their own insecurities or social conditioning, and they don't have a say in your life.

It's time to fucking free yourself.

Live for you.

~ ~ ~

Trusting your intuition brings you closer to your true self. It's like learning to trust your inner compass, even when it doesn't align with what society or the outside world expects from you. When you stop drinking, your intuition, or inner voice, will become stronger. Your intuition may first emerge as a very quiet soul whisper, easily drowned out by the noise of daily life. You may not even recognize it at first. But as you create space for stillness and tune into its frequency, that whisper will be grounded steps in alignment with what it's telling you. Sometimes, intuition can feel "crazy" because it doesn't always follow logic or the neatly structured patterns that society values. Intuitive hits can be sudden, irrational, or seemingly out of nowhere— sometimes contradicting what we've been taught or what the people around us believe. It's natural to second-guess yourself, to wonder if you're imagining things. Just keep listening. Throughout history, many people who were labeled "crazy" were actually the visionaries— the real geniuses, the true changemakers, ahead of their time.

I encourage you to *LISTEN TO YOUR INTUITION WITHOUT ANY OUTSIDE INFLUENCE AND TO TRUST IT BEFORE IT MAKES SENSE.*

The more you honor your intuition, the more it will reveal, like an exciting feedback loop. It's like developing a relationship— one built on presence, patience, and practice. You don't need to explain it to anyone, justify it, or make it palatable for others. The truth is, your intuition is not up for debate. It's not a group project. It's a sacred channel between you and your highest self. And sometimes, trusting it means walking away from things that *look good on paper* but feel *off* in your bones. Let that be enough.

But What if I Screw Up?

You're not going to. The real screw up is doing nothing and continuing to do the same old shit, different day.

When you make big decisions to step away from your old life, it's important to remember that they're rarely as final as they feel. More often than not, you can always choose to return to your comfort zone. This understanding can take some of the fear out of those seemingly monumental choices.

Change can be scary. You finally work up the courage to take the leap, you're momentarily suspended in mid-air, and your safe landing no longer looks like a sure thing. It can be a real "oh shit!" moment. Just give yourself some grace. You've come a long way. Remember that what you were doing **wasn't working anymore**, or you wouldn't even be here. And who's to say you won't make a perfect landing? I'm betting on you and cheering you on.

After getting mostly sober, realizing that I didn't want to live in NYC anymore, and working in the film industry no longer made my soul happy, of *course*, I was terrified to make a change. I was leaving it all behind and jumping into the unknown. Initially, I thought I would keep my apartment in Brooklyn, planning to sublet it to a friend. Two months before I left, the universe had different plans for me. That friendship completely fell apart in the strangest, almost fated-like way, and I essentially had two options: *force* the sublet, or *surrender* to what was unfolding naturally. My intuition was telling me to *let the apartment go* instead of finding another person to sublet, and I instantly felt lighter and freer when considering that decision. Now, I couldn't even imagine still being tethered to that apartment by way of my name on a lease. New York energy feels so wrong for me, and I am more than thankful I do not have to go back to deal with any bullshit like that.

Secondly, I took a chance and walked away from my highest-paying job yet, living off my savings to figure out something new. I have survived on that much longer than I originally anticipated, because abundance has presented itself in many forms, including a couple of very cheap living situations. When we notice that abundance comes in many forms, not just income or the number of dollars sitting in the bank, we can be grateful for so much more.

I thought I never wanted to sew again, because the demands of the film industry seriously sucked the fun right out of it for me. But with time and space to create again (yet *another* form of abundance!) from a place of true creativity, new designs have been flowing out of me. It's interesting to observe how my talent is manifesting in completely different ways now, such as in a new collection that is spiritually aligned or teaching at a local art gallery.

My point is, if you are doing something in alignment with your authenticity, it will never be a "screw up." **Nothing real can be threatened.** The universe will co-create with you to make it even better than you imagined. If it makes you feel better, keep one foot on the land while you navigate new waters (just as I did with potentially keeping my apartment). Then take the baby steps into deeper waters until you are comfortable swimming on your own.

~ ~ ~

The concept of "failure" should be erased from our vocabulary. "Failure" is never truly the end. It's simply a stepping stone, bringing lessons and wisdom and sometimes leading you down a new, more aligned path. "Failure" reveals when something isn't meant for you, but often, it clears space for something even better.

Think about a time when you thought you "failed" or had a "negative" experience, and look at the positive outcomes that emerged. Life has a way of balancing itself, and no matter what happens, you always have the power to shift your perspective. Trust that the universe knows what it is doing and has your best interest in mind, as long as you are living in alignment with your truth.

One day, on my travels after leaving New York, I re-experienced the childlike joy of doodling, something I hadn't done for years, which brought me into a meditative, receptive state. I received a message that stuck with me deeply: "There are no wrong answers. Every way is perfect." This simple yet powerful wisdom shifted my entire perspective. It reminds me that every decision we make is the right one, even if we can't see it in the moment.

Life isn't about making "perfect" choices; it's about the journey those choices take us on. Every path, every turn, every seemingly "wrong" decision brings with it an opportunity for growth, learning, and self-discovery. The only way something becomes negative is by choosing to label it that way. The truth is, even the challenges and mistakes are just part of the perfect unfolding of our lives. They're not failures— they're lessons, each with a valuable purpose, contributing to our ultimate growth and understanding. The key is to embrace the process with openness and trust, knowing that every experience, no matter how it appears on the surface, is guiding us exactly where we need to be.

Starting over without alcohol can feel like being dropped into unfamiliar territory without a map or a clear sense of direction. Over time, though, I've collected a handful of insights— practical, spiritual, and intuitive— to help me navigate. For these tools to help guide the process, please refer to *Support Tools 4: Tricks to Navigate a New Life.*

The Search for Purpose

Through the course of my healing journey, I've uncovered a significant truth about my past relationship with alcohol: it was a way to numb the deep dissatisfaction and emptiness I felt from not feeling like anything I was doing was worth a fuck. It was as if I were disconnected from the core of who I am, unable to tap into that deeper well of meaning and fulfillment. What was I here to *do, really?* Because there's no fucking way that I agree to believe I incarnated on this spinning marble just to pay bills and die of capitalism. When I stopped drinking and the muddy water cleared, I was able to see how shallow my pond was. The search for greater depth and purpose became a driving force, propelling me toward the conviction that life was meant to be more than the mundane cycle of work, routines, and fleeting pleasures.

However, as I've dove deeper into healing, I've discovered that purpose doesn't always announce itself in grand, obvious ways. Instead, it's often a gentle unfolding— like a seed slowly sprouting in the soil. Through this process, I've learned that purpose is less about achieving some external goal or destination and more about leaning into who I inherently am. It's about recognizing those aspects of myself that feel natural, those things I'm drawn to, and surrendering to them rather than resisting them out of fear or doubt. The more I embrace these intrinsic parts of myself, the more things begin to flow effortlessly— like the universe is conspiring to align me with the life I'm meant to live.

Our purpose is often already inside us, waiting to be uncovered. It's a process of stripping away the layers of conditioning, fear, and distraction that keep us from seeing it. It's not always an immediate revelation or something to be found "out there" in the world. Sometimes, it's simply the quiet knowing that when we stop fighting who we are and start honoring it, we begin to see the path unfolding before us, baby step by baby step.

In learning to surrender to my truth, the search for purpose no longer feels like a frantic chase but more like an invitation to be present with the ebb and flow of life. By honoring the unique qualities that make me who I am, I feel more connected, more aligned, and, most importantly, more whole. By taking action in ways that are truly aligned with your soul, you will naturally bring more soul into what you are doing, therefore, more meaning.

The deeper I dive into my purpose, the more I realize that this journey isn't about reaching a singular destination but rather about embracing each moment as it is, knowing that the steps I take today are leading me to exactly where I need to be. The search for purpose is not an endpoint— it's a lifelong unfolding of who we are meant to become.

There is no need to hurry. You are in perfect divine timing.

Please refer *to Support Tool 5* for resources that can help you recognize your purpose.

Part 5: Support Tools

Let's be real— this shit is hard. Choosing a different path, especially when that path means leaving behind the comfort of numbing, can feel like tearing off your skin in public and walking around exposed. There's no manual for this. No one hands you a playbook the day you stop drinking or start waking up to your own energy. You're just out there, raw and confused, trying to hold it together while your old life crumbles and something new, unfamiliar, and hopefully better starts to take shape.

This section isn't about rules or dogma. It's a collection of tools that helped me survive the chaos of early sobriety, the ache of shedding my old identity, and the deep hunger to feel *real* again. These are podcasts I binged while walking alone, rituals that grounded me when I thought I was losing my mind, and spiritual hacks that reminded me of who I am— at a time when everything felt too confusing.

You don't have to use all of them. You don't have to believe in all of them. But if even one of these tools gives you a moment of clarity, a pause in the spiral, or a sense that maybe, just maybe, you're not alone in this... then it's worth sharing.

Use what works. Toss the rest. And remember— you're not broken. You're just waking up.

Support Tool 1: Media

If you can't stop thinking about drinking, don't fight it— lean into it and analyze the hell out of it. After all, drinking was an obsession for so long, and wanting to understand every aspect as part of gaining control is completely normal. Here are some podcasts, "Quit Lit," and groups that helped me during the first 3–6 months of my journey. There's plenty more out there, but these are the ones that resonated with me:

Podcasts

- *Sober Powered* – Great short tidbits of scientific information

- *Andrew Huberman: What Alcohol Does to Your Brain and Body* – This info is shocking.

- *Sobriety Uncensored Podcast* – Entertaining, relatable shit talking

Books:

- The Unexpected Joy of Being Sober

- The Naked Mind

Groups:

- Sober Curious (Facebook)

- Sober.NYC (WhatsApp)

Support Tool 2: Craving Journal Prompts

Cravings don't just show up out of nowhere— they're messengers. They often carry information about how we're *really* doing beneath the surface. This is where you have to get brutally honest with yourself. No filters, no bullshit. Because if you don't name it, it'll keep running the show from the shadows.

- How am I feeling today in general? Why?

- What do I not prefer about today?

- What events led to this craving?

- Why do I want to drink?

- Is there an underlying need asking to be filled? What is behind that need?

- What emotions are coming up for me at this moment? Why?

- Who have I been around today that could be connected to this craving?

- Are these emotions my own? Or am I carrying someone else's emotions?

- What could I do differently to reduce this same trigger if it happens again?

Support Tool 3: Energetic Hygiene Practices

These practices are here to help you clear out what isn't yours. You're picking up other people's energy all day— your friend who trauma-dumped before noon, your partner's bad mood, the coworker who sighed 47 times, and that one subway screamer. It's no wonder you feel off. These practices help you clear your energetic space so that you can feel *your* feelings, not everyone else's. You'll feel more grounded, less foggy, and way more like yourself. The more you personalize your practice to what feels right to *you*, the better it's going to work for you. With practice, you will be able to ground, clear, and protect yourself in a matter of seconds, anytime, anywhere.

Grounding and Protection Basics:

1. **Energetically connect to the earth.** I start every day with a simple grounding ritual. Weather and circumstances permitting, I like to do this outside, barefoot and standing or sitting on the ground or in the shower. After closing my eyes and taking a few deep cleansing breaths, I imagine a beam of red light stretching from my root chakra to the center of the earth. On other days, I might picture my legs and feet growing deep roots into the soil or a red rope tied around my waist, anchoring me securely to the earth's core. Whatever feels right that day is what I go with. Whenever I have the opportunity during my day, I'll physically connect barefoot to the Earth, or when it's not conducive to be outside, I'll use a grounding mat and/or grounding sheets— these were especially useful products when I lived in a city with not much natural space.

2. Clear your energy. I imagine the water from my shower washing away any negativity from my body and energy field. Sometimes, I picture myself bathing in the salty ocean or standing on a windy cliff, letting the wind sweep away any stagnant or heavy energy. To physically enhance the process, I use a homemade combination of Dead Sea salt or Epsom salt mixed with coconut oil to wash my body. I like to smudge myself and my space with sage or palo santo whenever I need some extra clearing. Sage and Palo Santo are a little different. Sage is stronger and neutralizes all energy, good and bad. Palo Santo is more gentle and uplifting.

3. Protect your auric energy field. I visualize a beam of white light entering through my crown chakra, filling me from the inside out, and radiating until my entire body and aura are made of pure white light. This light extends about three feet around me, creating a protective shield. While doing this, I say the words "light up" to set my intention. At other times, I might imagine myself drawing protective circles around my energy field or being surrounded by an energetic, geometric crystal shape, such as a Merkabah, to feel even more secure.

Support Tool 4: Tricks to Navigate a New Life

Navigating a new life can feel confusing and overwhelming, but along the way, I've picked up a few gems of wisdom that have helped me tremendously. These aren't rigid rules or universal solutions, but gentle offerings. Take what resonates, leave what doesn't, and trust that your inner wisdom will guide you forward. You're more capable than you think.

The Follow Your Excitement Formula by Bashar

- **Step 1:** Act on your excitement, your passion, what is most exciting to you, in the moment. Do this every moment that you can.

- **Step 2:** Do this to the best of your ability. Take it as far as you can go until you cannot take it any further.

- **Step 3:** Act on your excitement/passion with absolutely no insistence, assumption, or expectation on what the outcome should be.

- **Step 4:** Choose to remain in a positive state regardless of what happens.

- **Step 5:** Constantly investigate your belief systems. Release and replace the un-preferred beliefs: fear-based beliefs, and the beliefs not in alignment with who you prefer to be.

Yes or No Intuition

Your body knows the answers if you can get comfortable tuning in. No question is too big or too small.

First, close your eyes and take a few deep breaths to arrive at a comfortable, relaxed standing position. Connect energetically to the earth, as described in *Support Tool 3*. Hands at your sides, or maybe connect them to your heart, whatever feels right for you.

Ask your body to *"show me a yes."* Notice any sensations your body gives you. Where in your body do you feel it? For me, I sway slightly forward, like a magnetism towards the subject of the question. My shoulders draw slightly back, my heart forward, and my chin up— all mimic confident body language.

Ask your body to *"show me a no,"* and take note in the same way. For me, I sway slightly back like I'm energetically being pushed away from the question, shoulders round forward, and chin points down. It's like I am hiding from the question and want to slink away without being noticed. I notice a heaviness or a pit in my stomach when it feels wrong.

Build trust with this method by starting with small questions, such as deciding what to eat or drink, and work your way up to the bigger questions.

Fork in the Road Meditation

When faced with a decision, sometimes I'll picture it as a fork in the road. I take a moment to sit quietly, visualizing myself on each path of the possible paths ahead. I imagine what my life would look like and how each choice would make me feel, allowing myself to experience both possibilities fully. After fully immersing myself in what the experiences might look and feel like for me, I tune into my gut for an intuitive answer about which path to take. This can even be used for something as simple as "Should I go to yoga class or not?" You may find that a self-care pity party may be better for you in the moment.

51% Rule

The 51% rule refers to the idea that you never have to be 100% yes or no on any decisions before you take action. Only 51%. It's better to take any action than be stagnant for too long.

To take it a step further, creating meaningful change or transformation in your life requires shifting your thoughts, feelings, or actions by only 51%. In other words, it's not about being perfect or always doing things "right," but rather tipping the scale toward a positive direction. If more than half of your energy is aligned with your goals, values, or desired outcomes, you are already on the path to success.

Pendulum Work

When I face a difficult decision, I sometimes use a pendulum to seek clarity and guidance from my higher self, guides, or insight into my subconscious mind. Many metaphysical shops carry pendulums, but you can also make one out of a crystal or stone suspended on about 6 inches of chain or string, or even use a necklace. Choose one that feels energetically aligned with you.

1. Find a quiet place where you will not be disturbed
2. Ground, clear, and protect yourself. (*Support Tool 3*)
3. Hold the pendulum in your right hand, with your elbow close to your side to reduce movement.
4. Hold your left palm about one inch under the bottom of the pendulum.
5. Hold the pendulum as still as possible.
6. Ask the pendulum, "Show me a Yes," and observe if it moves forward-back, side-to-side, or in a circle, clockwise or counter-clockwise, and take note.
7. Ask "Show me a No," and see how it differs.
8. "Show me a Maybe"
9. Ask if any of your guides would like to speak with you.
10. Ask clear "yes or no" questions, starting with simple things you know the answer to, to build trust.
11. Give gratitude for the answers.

Get Clear With What You Want

Manifestation is a co-creative process between you and the universe. Imagine the universe as an intricate web of energy, constantly responding to the frequencies you emit. Your thoughts, emotions, and actions are all signals you send out, shaping the reality you experience.

If your intentions are unclear, scattered, or contradictory, the universe mirrors that confusion back to you. It's like placing an order at a restaurant but changing your mind halfway through— how can the kitchen prepare what you want if you don't even know? The same applies to your life. When you lack clarity, you receive mixed results, reinforcing feelings of uncertainty and stagnation.

But when you set clear, intentional goals and align your energy with them, the universe conspires to bring them into your reality. If you focus on abundance, gratitude, and possibility, you'll naturally attract more of those things. If you dwell in lack, fear, and doubt, you'll continue to see those reflections in your life.

The way that Joe Dispenza describes these concepts from a scientific perspective in his book *Becoming Supernatural* blew my mind. I am a big fan of his meditations.

Meditating and visualizing your ideal future, creating vision boards, journaling in the present tense as if your manifestations are already happening, or stating affirmations and mantras daily are all great ways to align with your highest timeline. There are so many ways to do this— do what feels right to you.

Micro-Manifesting

Sometimes, we don't know what we want in a bigger, overarching sense, and that's ok! In that case, start smaller. Micro-manifesting is the subtle yet powerful process of directing your energy toward your desires in small, intentional ways every day. We do it constantly, often without realizing it.

Remember when I talked about our bodies being antennas in *The Spiritual Effects of Alcohol*? We attract similar vibrations to what we are. Manifesting is the law of attraction. Whether it's focusing on gratitude for what you have or making choices that align with your higher self, we are manifesting on a micro level every moment. The key is to be conscious of where you're placing your energy. Every thought, action, and emotion sends vibrations into the universe, contributing to the creation of your reality, matching the same vibration.

For example, we choose to nourish ourselves with a healthier choice at a restaurant rather than an unhealthy one. We choose to see the positive side of a situation rather than the negative. We choose a small act of kindness in a situation where we would appreciate the same. Over time, these small decisions will ultimately lead to greater overall alignment.

When we deliberately channel our energy toward our highest good, we're creating a stream of focused intention. This doesn't mean we have to make grand gestures or take massive leaps all at once. It's about being aware of the small decisions—where we choose to focus, how we react, who we spend time with, and what we put our attention on. When we prioritize alignment with our goals, values, and vision for our best life, we begin to micro-manifest the outcomes we desire. Over time, these little actions compound and form the foundation of larger manifestations. Think of it like steering a ship: if we're consistently turning the wheel just a few degrees in the right direction every day, we'll eventually be on course for our destination. Similarly, by consistently putting energy into positive actions, thoughts, and intentions, we create a life that is aligned with our highest good— one micro-manifestation at a time. In time, a bigger picture will become clearer.

Human Design

Please refer to *Support Tool 6: Human Design* for a holistic overview of the system. Your Strategy and Authority are suggestions on how to navigate life.

Support Tool 5: Clues to Discovering our Purpose

Numerology Life Path Number

Your Life Path number in numerology is calculated by adding up the digits of your birthdate until you get a single-digit number (or one of the "master numbers" 11, 22, or 33). This number reveals the core of your personality, your purpose, and the challenges or lessons you're meant to work through in this lifetime. There are lots of websites that offer numerology calculators and explanations.

Numerology Name Number

In numerology, your name number, also known as your destiny number, is a number that's calculated from your full name. It's said to reveal your life's purpose, strengths, and potential. Your name number represents your life potential, personality traits, and natural talents. It is calculated by adding up the numbers associated with each letter of your full name at birth. Plenty of websites will do the calculation for you.

Astrology

There are a few key placements in our astrological charts that give us insight into aligning with our purpose. Again, I recommend getting a professional reading to see how it all ties together. However, you can easily generate your chart and look up the meanings of these placements online. Including the degree placement reveals even deeper insight. For example, search or type into an AI-assisted program: *What does my [insert planet/node] in [insert sign] at [insert degree number] degrees in the [insert house number] house mean, and how does this connect to my higher purpose?*

Sun Sign and House - Core Identity and Purpose

- Your sun sign represents your core essence and the qualities you are meant to embody in this life.
- The house your sun is in shows where you shine the most and where your energy is focused.

North Node and South Node - Karmic Path and Soul Mission

- The north node is your life's purpose, growth, and soul's direction, where you are meant to evolve, even if it feels uncomfortable at first.
- The south node represents your past life traits, comfort zone, and natural abilities, but staying here too much can keep you stuck.

Midheaven (MC) - Career and Public Legacy

- This shows your highest potential, career path, how you are seen in the world, and what you are meant to contribute.

Part of Fortune - Natural Flow and Success

- This shows where you experience luck, joy, and fulfillment when aligned with your purpose.

Human Design

Please refer to *Support Tool 6: Human Design* for a holistic overview of the system. The Personality Profile, Sun Gate, and Incarnation Cross are deep clues to discovering our purpose.

Gene Keys Hologenetic Profile

The Gene Keys Hologenetic Profile is a profound system of self-discovery that builds upon the concepts of Human Design, delving deeper into your genetic coding. It's a unique system designed by Richard Rudd, focusing on unlocking your higher potential, understanding the shadow aspects of your personality, and ultimately allowing you to live a life aligned with your highest truth.

In essence, the Gene Keys Hologenetic Profile is a map of your soul's journey, outlining your purpose, challenges, emotional healing, and how you can move towards your highest most aligned expression. It's not just about understanding your personality traits but also unlocking deep wisdom hidden within your genetic structure. The system is about unlocking your potential and living from a place of grace, flow, and wisdom. The free chart can be generated online.

Support Tool 6: Human Design

When I discovered Human Design, my whole world started to make sense. Of all the systems, tools, or resources mentioned in this book, Human Design has been the most influential and profound in my personal journey. Human Design is like your instruction manual, describing how to navigate life in a way that works best for your unique energy. Through understanding our unique BodyGraphs, we reduce self-judgment and allow our life purpose to flow through us.

Human Design is a synthesis of several systems (Quantum Physics, Biochemistry, Astrology, the Hindu Chakra System, Kabbalah, and the Chinese I Ching). When combined, the result transcends each component. Our Human Design BodyGraph reveals our roles within the totality of humanity, enabling us to live in alignment with our true nature rather than conforming to societal norms. It allows us to take the correct action based on our unique energy type and decision-making authority.

The following few pages are a very basic overview. To generate your BodyGraph for free or see mine as an example, go to www.caseycrespo.com.

The *types* in Human Design make it clear that we are not all built the same way, and we are not here to function in the same way. With this understanding came a deep compassion for how I should navigate life, as well as how to interact with the people closest to me.

Type

In Human Design, there are four main energy types, or aura types. Generators, Projectors, Manifestors, and Reflectors. I would encourage you to research your Human Design type, because we are not all meant to use our energy in the same way. I love Human Design because it acknowledges our differences, rather than assuming we are all supposed to operate in the same way.

- **Generators** are the life force energy of the planet, and have the energy to work most of the day, assuming the work they're doing lights them up, and they have agreed to the projects that are correct for them.
- **Projectors** are here to guide, and do not have the same energy resource as Generators. They work very intensely and efficiently, but can feel incredibly drained if they work society's definition of a "normal" day. They need the most rest.
- **Manifestors** work in bursts of inconsistent energy, having focused energy on what lights them up, and then crashing.
- **Reflectors** energy fluctuates based on the energy they are surrounded by. They are here to be sacred mirrors of the collective, reflecting the health of the community.

Authority

The way we are designed to make decisions based on our unique type is called our "Authority." Our Authority is *never* our mind, and there are seven different authorities in Human Design— emotional, sacral, splenic, just to name a few. For example, I have a sacral authority, which means I respond to life with "uh-huh" or "uh-uh' (yes or no) responses, and these come from a gut feeling, not my mind. I encourage you to research "What does [insert your authority] in Human Design mean?" after generating your chart, where you can see your authority listed below the BodyGraph chart. Or, better yet, get a reading to understand how your chart works holistically.

Personality Profile

Your profile will look like two numbers. For example, mine is 3/5. This shows *how* you fulfill your purpose— it's like the costume you wear in life. There are 12 personality profiles.

Personality Sun Gate

Your Sun Gate is determined by the position of the Sun at the time of your birth, and it reveals the core energy and essence of who you are. This gate represents your natural strengths, challenges, and life's purpose, offering insight into your inner essence and how you are meant to express yourself in the world. When you generate your BodyGraph chart online, it is the first number on the right column. I encourage you to research this online for free.

Incarnation Cross

In Human Design, "fulfilling our purpose takes a lifetime of patient and disciplined attention to making decisions that are correct for us, combined with a dedication to fine-tuning our awareness" (from the Definitive Book of Human Design). The Incarnation Cross represents your life's purpose and how you're meant to express your energy in the world. When you generate your chart online, it will show you below what the name of your incarnation cross is, and you can research what it means for free.

Centers

Our BodyGraph charts provide valuable insights into how we interact with the world, including where we are most sensitive to external energies and conditioning. There are nine centers in Human Design, each an energy hub that transforms or transmutes the life force as it flows through the BodyGraph, represented as 'defined' (colored in) or 'undefined' (white). The areas in our charts that are 'undefined' or 'open' are where we're most vulnerable to influences outside of ourselves.

I would like to give an example of an aspect of one center here. Emotions, feelings, and sensitivity are expressed in the Solar Plexus Center, the center that is the farthest right triangle when looking at your BodyGraph. It is either open (undefined) or defined (colored in). If it is defined, you produce your own wave of emotions. If it is open, you absorb, amplify, and reflect the emotions of those around you. If it is open, this is the Human Design definition of an empath.

My chart is open or undefined in this area, revealing that I am highly sensitive to external influences and energies. My design enables me to absorb and amplify the emotions of others. With this realization, it became clear just how essential it is to distinguish which emotions are mine and which ones I need to release. Reflecting on my years of heavy drinking, I saw that I would often drink to try to numb or mask the emotions I was absorbing. Now, clearing these energies, as described in the *Support Tool 3: Energetic Hygiene Practices*, has become a vital part of my daily routine.

Support Tool 7: Herbal Inspiration

When I got mostly sober, I needed *something physical* to reach for— something that wasn't a bottle, a vice, or a downward spiral. Herbs became one of those somethings. They helped me manage my mood, support my nervous system, and reconnect with my body in a way that felt intentional. This isn't about chasing a high — it's about working with the earth instead of against yourself. That said, herbs aren't just cozy little plants in cute jars — they're powerful, and you should always do your research and check in with a doctor, especially if you're on medication. What follows are some of the herbal allies that supported me through the messier moments of early sobriety— from anxiety to gut imbalances to the need to feel just a little more connected to something bigger than me.

Feeling anxious? Kava.

In the first six months of getting mostly sober, I drank a lot of kava. It became a go-to for managing the flood of emotions that surfaced, along with the anxiety about what to do with them. Kava helped take the edge off and offered a sense of calm without the baggage that comes with alcohol. Please note that kava can be hard on the liver, so please research before consuming it. It's also important to note that kava is not the same as kratom, even though they're often offered side by side. While kava was helpful for me, I wouldn't recommend kratom— it's a completely different substance with its own set of risks and, in my opinion, feels very low-vibrational.

Need uplifting, positive energy? Turmeric (golden milk latte), ginger, lemon, lemongrass, ginseng.

Think of yellow things, like the sun, if you need a dose of positivity (side note: do you need some sun today??). Curcumin, the active ingredient in turmeric, has shown antidepressant effects in animal and human studies, and I sure can feel that when I consume it. Bright, zingy flavors like ginger and lemon have the same effect on me. The spice of ginger reminds me of fire, activating my life force energy. When my taste buds light up, my mood seems to follow suit!

Need a calm focus: matcha green tea for L-theanine

I developed an affinity (or maybe transfer addiction) for matcha while working, and upon deeper research, discovered why. L-theanine is an amino acid known for its calming effects. It's primarily found in green tea, matcha, and white tea, with matcha being the highest concentration. L-theanine may offer various health benefits, including improved mental focus and sleep quality. When taken with caffeine, L-theanine might boost alertness and concentration.

Feeling ungrounded or carrying unwanted energy? Palo santo and sage

Not just for burning. I like to shave some pieces of palo santo in my French press and steep for 5 minutes. Same with a few sage leaves (a little goes a long way). It's like smudging yourself from the inside out to clear your energy!

Feeling too harsh, assertive, or aggressive? Rose, chamomile, hibiscus, jasmine, lavender

I'm a woman, but sometimes my masculine and feminine energies feel out of balance, especially when the less helpful sides of my masculine energy start to show up. We should all strive to operate from a place of balance, regardless of our gender. To help restore this harmony, I often turn to floral teas, especially rose, which is associated with the heart chakra and carries a high vibrational, soothing, gentle, feminine energy. Chamomile has a calming, delicate energy. Hibiscus carries an uplifting, fiery energy. Jasmine is passionate and uplifting. Lavender is calming, soothing and protective.

Desire to enhance connection to the divine/my higher self, or the dream realm? Blue lotus

Blue lotus is not approved for human consumption in the United States. But in my opinion, alcohol shouldn't be either. Do your research. Blue Lotus is the second-highest vibrational flower on the planet, next to rose. A tea before bed raises my vibration and makes me have interesting and enlightening dreams.

Stomach/digestion feels unbalanced? Kombucha, kefir, peppermint, and apple cider vinegar

Your gut flora is so important to your overall health, and when you stop drinking, it's going to need some help to level itself back out. Apple cider vinegar in some soda water has an interesting combination of bite, tang, and a hint of something unpleasant, reminiscent of our favorite alcoholic drinks; enjoy! Try different kombuchas, make it fun, and have your own tasting at home. I've even seen kombucha bars popping up!

Need a whole body reset? Detox herbs like milk thistle, dandelion, and fennel

When I want to be extra kind to my body, I go for a pre-made detox tea blend instead of sourcing all the herbs individually. I'll even make it iced and add some lemon and honey and sip it throughout the day. Milk thistle is especially good for the liver, after all the abuse we put it through.

Part 6: "Go to the Desert"

I knew that I had to empty my life to make room for the new. That's what this entire journey has become about. The internal guidance telling me what was not right for me was louder than any nudges to make bigger, long-term decisions. So, I felt the need to *edit things out* of my life before I could *add to it*. I knew what things felt misaligned and inauthentic, but I didn't have a vision for my new future just yet. I needed to step back and look at the bigger picture, step out of the frame completely, pick a new frame to paint a new picture in, and then re-enter it with tiny baby steps.

But I had no idea what those baby steps would be. When I left New York to begin a new path, I completely surrendered— to the universe, to the empty void of nothingness that was simultaneously full of infinite possibilities. I surrendered to my intuition. To the trust that my higher self would guide me exactly where I needed to go. I believed the net would appear when I jumped. So, I jumped.

A month after I started writing this book, and eight months before I left New York, the shaman from the sacred plant ceremony that had kicked off my sobriety appeared to me in an incredibly vivid, profound, yet brief dream and told me, **"Go to the desert."** It was so authoritative that I wanted to drop everything I was doing and take a trip to the desert immediately. I don't take dreams lightly. I also took this statement as a metaphor for staying dry from alcohol, and so it became the title of this book. But it still felt like advice to be taken *literally*, and as my plans shaped up to leave New York, I was pulled to the desert. Little did I know how the symbolism of the desert would continue to tie into my self-development, along with the progression of this book.

There is immense symbolism and wisdom within dreams if we are open to receiving it. They can be messages from our higher selves, glimpses into our subconscious, reflections of trauma that need healing, or guidance to help us navigate life. The more you pay attention to and honor the guidance from your higher self, the universe, or source, the more it continues to reveal.

I'm writing this final chapter in the heart of the Sonoran Desert. If I tried to explain to most people how I got here, it likely wouldn't make sense in the language of small talk.

~ ~ ~

My time in New York was done. I had always wanted to experience it, and I did. I had "made it," reaching the top of my industry and living alone comfortably for the last two years— a goal that I had set for myself. Chapter complete. Check. I knew I wanted to leave, but I had no idea where to go. What I *did* know was that I was tired of the endless cycle— working to make rich people richer while pouring most of my money into an apartment I would never own. There had to be a better way, and I was determined to find it. Cutting alcohol out of my life lifted the veil. It stripped away the numbness, making it harder— no, impossible— to stay complacent in a life that no longer made any fucking sense to me.

So, it was about halfway through my last film job in New York that I decided that purchasing and living in a home on wheels would be the best decision for me. I planned my transition for when my lease ended, which just so happened to align perfectly with the end of my job— another synchronistic gift from the universe. I knew nothing about any of it. Did I need a van, an RV, a truck, or a truck with a pull-behind camper? For me, there's no way of knowing what I need until I experience something. So, I handed the task of finding my new home to a good friend whose expertise I trusted, and I surrendered to whatever the universe decided was right for me. I bought my setup without even seeing it in person.

I am writing this from my 1991 20-foot pull-behind camper, sitting beside my 1998 truck. It's definitely nothing fancy, but it's what I could afford. If I had waited for some version of "perfect" that my mind wanted to make up, I'd probably still be waiting. Strangely enough, my years in New York— living in tiny apartments— unknowingly prepared me for this. It's comfortable, cozy, and has shown me just how little I actually need on a day-to-day basis. My life right now is incredibly simple.

I did a complete 180-degree turn— going from one of the most high-energy places on the planet, New York City, to being completely alone in the vast, barren expanse of the desert. My soul *needed* it. I had to shake off that New York energy, which had felt out of alignment for the last year and a half of my time there. Living amongst the concrete and right angles in NY was suffocating me.

Now, living in my camper, I'm more connected to the natural world than ever before. Since becoming mostly sober and embracing my sensitivity rather than numbing it, I've become acutely aware of the energies around me, including the collective energy of entire cities. New York's energy is fast-paced, hustle-driven, work-forward, and party-forward. It was exactly what I wanted when I first moved there. But as I got mostly sober, it became clear how deeply misaligned it was with my true, authentic self. The constant buzz of that collective energy overwhelmed me daily, until the only thing that made sense was to strip it all away— to exist with *almost no* outside energetic influence. To rediscover what my own energy even felt like. And so, I ended up in the desert.

What do *I* need? Without any outside influence. This work is not easy, but I felt called to do it. To strip away society's conditioning. To be reduced down to only my truest, most authentic self. To find what I had been hiding from for so long.

And just when I thought I had surrendered enough, the universe gave me even more. I didn't *choose* to be without cell service, but that's what I was handed. So, I surrendered to an even deeper level of solitude. And then, despite my near-total disconnection, the news still found me— a friend in New York had passed. In that moment, I became one with the barren landscape around me— a completely empty vessel.

~ ~ ~

The first few days in the desert, I felt this nagging need to *do* something, even though I had nothing to do and had arrived exactly where I supposedly wanted to be. Where was this pressure even coming from? I didn't understand it at first, but then it hit me: the pressure was the deep-rooted conditioning of capitalism that had been ingrained in me my entire life.

From a young age, we're sent to school nearly every day, assigned homework to fill our "free" time, only to graduate directly into the workforce, where overtime is expected in some cases. We spend our lives making rich people richer, funneling our money back into the very companies we work for. On top of that, we're constantly bombarded with advertisements telling us that we need to buy things to look a certain way or achieve some level of social status.

By removing myself from any city and cutting off access to social media, the internet, and even random ads you see everywhere in cities, I freed myself from those advertisements. I was finally able to ask myself what I truly needed on a daily basis, rather than letting the consumer-driven world dictate it to me. And what I found is that I need very, very little.

Deconditioning from that busy mindset— and accepting the stillness and simplicity— was tough. But I'm not working for *them* anymore. I'm working for and on *myself* through stillness and simplicity, and consciously choosing what I consume or add back in my life.

I also wanted to run away. I'd arrived at a place that didn't feel quite right— "my people," whatever that meant to me at the time, weren't there. I felt the urge to run, as it seemed like the next best thing to drinking, which would've been my go-to in the past. *What the fuck am I even doing here?* I paused, just as I had taught myself to pause before reacting in my *Craving Scenarios*. Where was I going to run to? Another situation where I wouldn't fit in? In 40 years on this planet, I've never truly felt like I fit into this world, so why would that change with just one more move to another campsite in another town?

I had to learn to be okay with not "fitting in" anywhere, and doing that required profound self-love and self-acceptance. I realized that I am truly the only one who needs to understand and love myself. The depth of my life and my needs can never be fully explained to another person, so I must ensure that those needs are met. I am whatever I need to be for myself. I am my own parent, my own sister I never had, my own best friend, my own lover.

And then, suddenly, the "not fitting in anywhere" dialogue shifted to: *I can be happy anywhere.*

I finally started to get it. I had spent my whole life running from myself— constantly searching for the next thing, something to do, another town to move to, someone to be interested in, external validation— all the while missing the truth that everything I need is already within me. It feels like this little gold nugget that sits right around my solar plexus. Whenever I need love, inner wisdom, or comfort, I can pull from it. It's my true center, my source. The more I interact with it, validate it, and give it love, the more it grows.

I surrendered to the slow pace of life. The simplicity of the landscape cleared my mind. What appeared to be a barren landscape was full of hidden beauty if I just paid attention. The landscape, which at first seemed to be one solid color, revealed a rainbow of rocks upon closer inspection. As I looked even more closely, I started finding sparkly geodes, which seemed to manifest at the same time as nuggets of wisdom from the desert.

Every now and then, the vast emptiness would be broken by a singular, gigantic cactus— the only one for miles— making it feel incredibly special and symbolic. Even seemingly small interactions with my neighbors grew more meaningful because we were sharing this unique human experience. The place was slowly growing on me. I know I won't be here forever, but right now, I'm incredibly grateful for it.

Everything I need is right here, right now, within me. Suddenly, the little gold nugget inside me began to expand into my heart, amplifying its power and radiating its beautiful golden light far beyond my physical body. I was no longer barren, but with a heart so full it needed to be shared with the world again.

I started to open up to my neighbors energetically. Coming from New York, this wasn't exactly natural— in fact, ignoring people in your general vicinity is more so the norm. But if we are living in a camper in the middle of the desert together, we all have at least one thing in common: we aren't doing things the way everyone else does. In the short time I have been living this lifestyle, I have observed a redefinition of what community can look like. Free yoga classes, bonfires under the full moon, random invites for hikes, the pure childlike joy of sharing our daily rock finds, neighborhood fires, sweet gifts being left on my door, even things I had lost being personally returned to me.

One day, I got stuck inside my camper because the heat had caused my doorknob to expand. When I yelled out my window for help, six of my neighbors came to my rescue, and my heart exploded from the support. Observing this community has given me incredible insight into how I'd like to move forward in life.

With the buffer of alcohol gone, I've realized I've spent most of my life bending over backward for jobs that weren't right for me, relationships that weren't right for me, and friendships that weren't right for me. Now, I'm using this time to reflect on my values and what I want my life to look like when I step back into it. What do I value most? What boundaries do I need to set? Whose energy am I going to allow to intertwine with mine? How can I be more present and aware of what's going on around me? And how can I carry this connected, grounded, authentic feeling with me as I move through life?

This is the time to be very intentional about how I want to move forward—with elevated emotions, clear intentions, and a deep-rooted need to live authentically and with integrity. I am no longer moving through life behind the mask of alcohol: mindlessly, without purpose, muffled, robotic, and sad. I am choosing a path that reflects who I truly am, and it feels like a sense of freedom is setting in.

I believe that taking time for yourself and caring for the health of your energetic field is one of the most important things you can do— not just for yourself but for the health of the planet. Our thoughts, emotions, and feelings influence our energy field, and that energy field has a domino effect on the collective consciousness. It is our duty to keep it healthy. However, for someone whose life is set up in such a way that they're giving a lot of their time to family, friends, work, and other obligations, taking time for yourself might seem selfish. But please understand that it is not selfish— it is selfless. The fuller your cup is, the easier it will be to share that abundance with others.

Alcohol lowers our vibrations, which in turn prevents us from moving through life on our highest, most abundant timelines. By working through the lessons we couldn't integrate while under the influence of alcohol, we allow ourselves to move forward— not just individually, but collectively. Each step we take toward healing and higher consciousness contributes to the collective energy, helping raise the vibration of the world around us.

It's time for us to create the things we wish existed. We have the power to create our own utopia. We are more powerful than we realize, creating our own reality with our thoughts and attracting the like, moment by moment. Our beliefs shape the world we live in— if we trust in this power, there's no limit to what we can create.

If we truly believe we are on the correct path to living our greatest life, then we are.

If we believe that everything happens for a reason and everything is working out in our favor, then it is.

If we believe that nothing in life is negative and everything carries a positive lesson, then it's true.

If we believe that we are divinely protected, then we are.

~ ~ ~

After two years of being mostly sober, I can now tell you that I feel physically high on life, no alcohol or drugs needed. This is what I was working towards, but it is not something I expected to experience so strongly. I seem to have psychedelic, other-worldly experiences almost every day by being in tune with the nuances of the beauty and magic of life instead of numbing them out. I experience mind-bending synchronicities every day. Signs from the universe are everywhere, and I'm choosing to pay attention to the magic and invite more of it in, fueling the most beautiful feedback loop.

Choosing to move through life without the daily influence of alcohol has transformed me in ways I never imagined. I'm deeply grateful for the opportunity to share my raw, real, and transformative journey, hoping it will inspire and guide others. We are all connected in this shared experience, and in embracing our truth, we awaken to the boundless possibilities that lie within and around us.

~ ~ ~

So here we are, at the end — or maybe the messy, beautiful, weird-ass beginning.

If you've made it this far, consider it proof: your **POWER** has been awakened. Something inside you is louder, braver, and more *you*.

You don't need to numb yourself to feel at home here on planet Earth. You belong here. You always did. Since your very first breath.

The magic was never in the bottle, the high, or the escape— it was always within you. And by now, you are remembering— you are the alchemist, capable of transformation. It's time to break out of that dark, restrictive fucking cocoon and let your wings breathe.

My wish for you is that you give yourself the same wild permissions I gave myself. To be fully human and fully divine at the same time. To fall apart and put yourself back together. To cry in the car and laugh five minutes later. To feel it all and not run. To stay awake to your own life.

To give yourself **SPACE** to figure out a different way.

To say **NO** instead of that people-pleasing yes.

To prioritize yourself and be unapologetic about it. To keep your vibration high, not just for your own well-being, but because your energy affects others— and that ripple effect helps lift the entire collective.

Maybe you're not all the way "there" yet. That's okay. There's no final destination, no trophy for spiritual perfection, no sober gold star. This path is sacred and deeply personal. You're processing the information presented in this book so that you may arrange it in a way that makes sense to you. My wish is that you now feel more equipped to walk it with grace and grit, grounded in your truth.

You've tasted what's possible when you choose presence over escape. You've gathered tools, support, and reminders that you can come back to anytime. You've met parts of yourself that were once hidden in the shadow, and maybe you even said, "Hey, you're kind of cool in a chaotic, unhealed inner-child way." That's growth.

This isn't the end. This is the part where you start writing your own damn story.

Be weird, be you, be free.
I love you.

Casey